Dr. Kimberlee Mendoza

Torrid Faith

40-Day Faith Challenge Devotional

Torrid Faith: 40-Day Faith Challenge Devotional
COPYRIGHT 2023 by Dr. Kimberlee Mendoza

Contact Information: titleadmin@pelicanbookgroup.com

All scripture quotations, unless otherwise indicated, are taken from the Holy Bible, New International Version(R), NIV(R), Copyright 1973, 1978, 1984, 2011 by Biblica, Inc.™ Used by permission of Zondervan. All rights reserved worldwide. www.zondervan.com

Scripture quotations, marked KJV are taken from the King James translation, public domain.

Scripture quotations marked DR, are taken from the Douay Rheims translation, public domain.

Scripture texts marked NAB are taken from the *New American Bible, revised edition* Copyright 2010, 1991, 1986, 1970 Confraternity of Christian Doctrine, Washington, D.C. and are used by permission of the copyright owner. All Rights Reserved. No part of the New American Bible may be reproduced in any form without permission in writing from the copyright owner.

Cover Art by *Nicola Martinez*

Crossover Books, a division of Pelican Ventures, LLC
www.pelicanbookgroup.com PO Box 1738 *Aztec, NM * 87410
Crossover Books and the Cross-and-Sun logo is a trademark of Pelican Ventures, LLC

Publishing History
First Crossover Books Edition, 2023
Paperback Edition ISBN 978-1-5223-0388-6
Published in the United States of America

INTRODUCTION

"You will seek Me and find Me when you seek Me with all your heart." (Jeremiah 29:13 NIV)

I became a Christian at age three, and with the exception of a two-year hiatus, I have served God for more than four decades. Twenty-eight of those years were in ministry. I have always attended church regularly, mid-week too, and tried to live a holy life by not cussing, partying—you know, all the usual stuff. And yet, I continued to struggle with some of the same sins. Gossip, a critical spirit, gluttony, apathy, the list goes on. Frustrated, I wondered why I never seemed to be any closer to God than I was the year before.

Then one summer, God grabbed my attention in an unusual way. For over thirteen years, my drama team and I had ministered at Teen Challenge. One night following a service, Teen Challenge invited us to a barbecue to thank us for our service. I had been asked almost every year but had never gone before. This time I decided to attend—a decision that would change my spiritual life forever.

In celebration of Teen Challenge's fiftieth anniversary, everyone at the barbecue was given the book, *The Cross and the Switchblade* by David Wilkerson—a true story about the author and how Teen Challenge began.

The story started with Wilkerson making the decision one night to turn off his TV and start praying instead. During that prayer time, God spoke to him. One night during his prayer time, he found himself distracted by an article on his desk about some gang members on trial in New York City. The Holy Spirit sparked something in him, and he decided to go see them. His insistence on seeing the men landed his picture in the newspaper and gave him instant notoriety among gang members—an "open door" that would allow him to minister to them almost immediately. His obedience not only reached the hearts of some of the hardest gang members at the time, but it has also spurred a worldwide organization (Teen Challenge) that saves thousands of lives each year.

I don't know why, but this story impassioned me. I was amazed at how one man's obedience could make such an enormous impact on millions of souls. Why was this man able to do so much for the Lord, and I struggled? The answer was almost too simple—time with God. Wilkerson made a conscious decision one day to turn off his TV and just pray.

After I finished reading his book, I decided to take the "Wilkerson challenge." Off went the television and the Internet for a month. I shut out the world for more than an hour every night and just spent time in devotion and prayer. And almost immediately, I began to see the fruits of this mission.

During my prayer time, I felt the call to finish applying to becoming a minister—a journey that I had stopped pursuing almost fifteen years prior due to some discouraging words. I didn't apply right away, but what I've discovered is that God doesn't just tell you something like that; He usually confirms it—especially if you need a nudge.

A few weeks later, I attended a retreat. The speaker, who didn't know my situation, started praying for me. She stopped and said, "Stop trying to get all your ducks in a row and just do what God has called you to do."

So, I filled out the application to be a minister. I would like to say I turned it in the very next day, but I didn't. I let it sit on my desk for several days, afraid once again of rejection. I used the excuse that financially, I just couldn't afford it. I prayed, "Lord, if you truly want me to do this, then you'll have to provide the $200.00 application fee."

My spouse called minutes later and said, "Did I tell you that I'm getting about $200 more in my paycheck?"

I sat wide-eyed and stunned. "OK, Lord, I get it." Finally, I obeyed and sent in my application. God walked me through the entire process. Each day was a new adventure, and I grew closer to Him, because I gave Him my time. My marriage was a hundred percent better, and I moved about in peace, despite some of the tough circumstances I walked through. My entire life took on a new and unexpected direction with several testimonies that will be explained later in this book.

The best part was that God's blessing didn't stop with me. I talked my youth group into doing the "Wilkerson Challenge" (or as I renamed it, "The Torrid Faith Challenge") and watched their lives also morph. Some of them were called into ministry themselves. Most were rapidly growing in their faith, down on their knees, making life-altering changes. In addition, some women and college kids who took "the challenge" reported that their lives were better and that they had found new purpose. I did this in an English class I was teaching, and students were stopping me after class to share amazing testimonies of how God had changed their lives.

Becoming too busy for a regular devotional life is a common pitfall for many modern Christians. I believe that revival in the church starts one life at a time. If you want to see growth in your life, then it starts in the most basic of places—time with God.

At one point, I was attending college, working several jobs, volunteering in four ministries, and had a family with two young sons. I knew "busy" well, but even in my busiest of moments, I managed to find time to eat. Why? Because if I didn't eat, my body would eventually grow weak and die. The same is true of the spiritual self. If we don't feed our spiritual body, eventually it will grow weak and die.

The number one reason why people tell me they can't take the challenge is because they are unable to give up one-hour of their day. Here is my four-point answer: 1) If you want to do this, you'll find yourself with extra time. 2) God would rather have you pray throughout your day, than make an appointment with Him at the end of the day, therefore, the hour can be spread over 24-hours. 3) The daily program will take up a big portion of the hour. 4) It is so important that you make God a priority.

God cares about our future, and us, but we need to spend time with Him so He can prepare us for it. You want to be on fire for God and in your faith—it starts with this spiritual challenge.

Hebrews 11:6b "He rewards those who sincerely seek Him."

TESTING FAITH

How hot is your fire really burning?

Take this test and be HONEST with yourself. Pick the one that MOST describes you. Don't feel discouraged but encouraged. This is the first step.

1. I usually...

   a. Read my Bible every day for more than twenty minutes
   b. Quickly read my Bible right before I go to bed
   c. Fit my devotion time in if I have a free moment
   d. Don't ever really read my Bible

2. I find...

   a. I talk to God as if He's my best friend for a good amount of time
   b. Sometimes I can pray only for five to ten minutes
   c. It is often difficult to find things to say during prayer time
   d. I never really talk to Him except when I have a problem

3. Which one of these sounds the most appealing?

   a. Going to a church revival on a week night
   b. Hanging out with friends
   c. Watching sports or TV
   d. Partying

4. Reading a devotional book...

   a. Changes my way of thinking

b. Isn't something I do often

c. Puts me to sleep

d. What's a devotional?

5. I have trouble with my mouth (cussing, gossiping, etc.)...

a. Never

b. Rarely

c. Sometimes

d. Always

6. Giving up the most important thing in my life for God...

a. Is easier every time, because I know the fruit of what will happen

b. Stings a bit, but I'm trying

c. Hurts and I'm not sure if I can do it

d. Not sure, I've never tried it

7. Prayer to me is...

a. As essential as eating

b. Important, but I could always do it more

c. Is something I do when I have problems

d. Something I don't do

8. If the pastor were to ask me to give up my favorite food and drink or hobby for a week, I would say...

a. Sure, I could do it

b. I'll pray about it

c. Sorry, can't right now

d. Forget it

9. When someone asks me to pray for them, I...

a. Start right then and there

b. Usually pray for them once or twice

c. Say I will, and then never do

d. People don't ask me to pray for them

10. I am reading this book because...

a. I'm just so on fire for God; I can't wait to get closer to Him

b. I would like to grow closer to God than I am now
c. Someone told me to or I was curious
d. I feel guilty

TALLY YOUR ANSWERS

Total number of A's: _____

Total number of B's: _____

Total number of C's: _____

Total number of D's: _____

CHECK YOUR FIRE LEVEL

If you had mostly A's, you are burning hot for God and by reading this book, you can hopefully find passion to ignite others.

If you had mostly B's, you're warm, but you have the right heart and with a little stirring of the ashes, you could ignite a blazing fire.

If you had mostly C's, you are lukewarm, and it's awesome that you're ready to read this book and get on fire for God. Note: I used to be a "C" until I took this challenge.

If you had mostly D's, you're a bit cold in your faith, but what better way to get warmer than to take this challenge.

The Challenge

Torrid means to be "hot and burning" and **faith** is your "walk and belief" as it applies to God. This book will hopefully help you become on fire for God.

For the next forty days, I challenge you to take the *Torrid Faith* Challenge. If you do, I believe your life *will* change. Who knows what God will do with and through you during this time? One man reported his life was 200% better after taking this challenge. A dozen or so others were called into full-time ministry.

You will get out of this challenge only what you put into it.

Some people look at the list of challenges and ask, "Why do I have to give up some of these things?"

The majority of the things I'm challenging you to give up are distractions. They are the "time and mind" robbers. I am not saying give them up for life (though some should probably go); I am just asking you to give them to God for the next forty days. If you're ready for your life to be better, you have to give in and let go of everything that is holding you back. If you're ready to be on fire for God, then you have to give in and let go of **everything**. The Holy Spirit is a gentleman; He won't force His way into your life. He will work in your life only as much as you let Him. So, do you want your life to be the best it can be? Are you willing to do all it takes to get there? Can you complete the challenge?

For the next forty days...

I will read my Bible and pray at least <u>one hour</u> a day. (Note: You can break this up into several segments, and an hour is no longer than one primetime TV show. The hour may include this workbook.)

I will work my way through this book.

I will refrain from watching any R-rated movies or raunchy PG-13 movies.

I will not listen to any secular music.

I will watch TV only seven hours <u>per week</u>. (Some people may want to go all in and not watch any TV for the challenge. I did, and it makes a difference.)

I will spend only <u>seven hours</u> playing on my computer or video games <u>per week</u>. (This does NOT include your job or homework. But you may consider cutting it out even more, everything you cut out during the 40-days makes a bigger difference).

I will abstain from drinking alcoholic beverages.

I will abstain from the use of any non-prescription drugs or smoking.

I will avoid cussing, foul talk, and gossip.

Unless married, I will not engage in any sexual activity.

I will tithe 10% of any money I make.

I will witness to someone in the next 40-days.

I will try to do at least one service project (feed a homeless person, buy a stranger's lunch, pick up trash, etc.)

I will fast at least <u>one meal</u> a week.

This is the challenge. You may alter as you see fit, but ask yourself why you are not able or willing to give up certain things. I know some people who will even add more specifics to their list. I challenge you to give the next 40-days (the time of new beginnings) to God.

TORRID FAITH:

YOUR PERSONAL
COMMITMENT

Torrid Faith COMMITMENT

I, _____, understand that this
is a 40-day commitment. I understand that I get out of this process
only what I put into it. For the next forty days, I will abstain from
drinking, drugs, cussing, sex (unless married), watching R-rated and
inappropriate PG-13 movies, and listening to secular music. I will
watch TV and/or play on the computer/game system for only seven
hours each week. I will tithe 10% of any money I make. I will pray for
those who don't know the Lord, and I will be an example worthy of
my calling as a follower of Christ.

Signed _____ Date _____

"Come near to God and he will come near to you..."
(James 4:8, NIV).

Torrid Faith:

The
Challenge
Begins

~ DAY 1 ~

GARBAGE IN

THEME: Feeding your Spirit
READ: Colossians 3:1-17

Have you ever played broomball? Broomball has to be one of the silliest ideas ever created. People step onto the ice in their tennis shoes with brooms in their hands and try to play hockey. With every step, people slip and toddle, hoping to stay upright. Inevitably, someone gets hurt. One summer, one of my youth leaders fell on the ice and hit his head. I didn't see it happen but watched as they carted him away in the ambulance. Later, we found out that he had been declared brain dead. As his wife agonized over whether to disconnect the machines, he began to hum worship songs. The doctors said he had absolutely no brain activity, and they could not explain this strange phenomenon.

His wife said it best, "It was his soul singing, not his brain."

What he had put into his soul came out. He was a godly man who worshipped the Lord daily. He loved Jesus with his whole heart. He loved to worship, and because he had fed his soul with good things, "good" poured out even when his body stopped working properly.

This made me rethink what I read, watched, and listened to daily. Consider for a moment, what would your soul pour out if it were suddenly the only thing left? I came to the conclusion that it does matter what we feed our minds, hearts, and souls. You've heard the old expression, garbage in, garbage out.

We each need to take an honest look at ourselves and our personal interests. Ask ourselves what is right and holy. We are called to live a holy life. We are called to examine our thoughts, words, and actions. We should shun evil and embrace what is good. I think too often we chalk sin up to "my guilty pleasure," or "everyone else is doing it" as if that makes it OK. I did this for years to give myself permission to watch whatever I wanted to watch on television. I gave myself permission to watch "trash TV," or listen to music full of sexual innuendo. I have found that as I cut those things out of my life, I am better for it.

It isn't my job to convince you of what is right and what is wrong. I can simply share my experience and show you what the Bible says about it. The Holy Spirit will be the judge of what path you decide to take. Just as He does for me. But I would encourage you to follow Philippians 4:8, "Finally, brothers and sisters, whatever is true, whatever is noble, whatever is right, whatever is pure, whatever is lovely, whatever is admirable—if anything is excellent or praiseworthy—think about such things."

God knows how powerful the temptations of this world are to our spirits. If we fill our hearts with worldly garbage, worldly garbage is what will come out. If we fill our heads with godly things, godly things will be what come out. As we strive for a better life, our effort must start with ridding those things that do not help our soul. I challenge you, at least for the next forty days, to give up an activity that you would not invite Jesus to do with you. You do not want anything that will distract you from this process. You just might find you didn't need it to begin with.

Thought:

"Whatever you put into your mind becomes part of the total you" (Zig Ziglar, 1926).

Action Step

Ask yourself: What are you feeding your soul? Junk food (those things that make you feel good, but are worldly) or healthy substances (the Bible, church, devotions, worship, etc.)? Write down those things that you should you probably get rid of. Could you do it for 40-days? Also, write down why or why not?

_____

_____

_____

_____

_____

_____

_____

_____

_____

Matt Redman - Heart of Worship
https://www.youtube.com/watch?v=OD4tB1o6YLw

Video Recommendation:

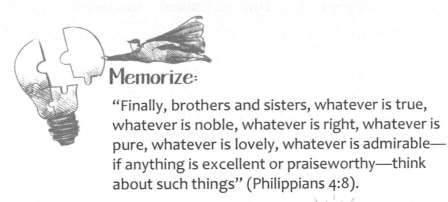

Memorize:

"Finally, brothers and sisters, whatever is true, whatever is noble, whatever is right, whatever is pure, whatever is lovely, whatever is admirable— if anything is excellent or praiseworthy—think about such things" (Philippians 4:8).

Pray

God, I pray as I start this journey, please speak to me about the things in my life that are in the way, that do not feed my soul. Give me the strength to get rid of them and find peace without them. Help me on this journey. Reveal Your will for my life and allow me to have a burning passion for the Word of God and doing Your will.

Write your own prayer:

_____

_____

_____

_____

_____

_____

_____

_____

_____

_____

~ DAY 2 ~

SERVING THE KING

THEME: Time with God
READ: Nehemiah 10:36-39

The tabloids love famous people, especially royalty. They follow every move out of Buckingham Palace. What new hat is the Duchess of Cambridge wearing? Where is Prince Harry going? What is Queen Elizabeth thinking? The press follow them everywhere, watching and waiting (and probably hoping) for them to do something questionable. They are famous enough that even Americans are fascinated by their lives.

If anyone of those reporters were invited into a royal's presence, they would not hesitate to go. If the Queen asked to come to your house, wouldn't you allow her to come, with great excitement? Consider what you would serve her when she got there. Would you pull out the leftovers in your fridge or would you make her the best meal possible? Chances are, you would either cater the dinner or dig out your best recipe with the finest ingredients. A meal fit for a queen, right? Why? Because she is important—she is royalty.

So, why do we often give Jesus, who is the King of Kings, our sloppy leftovers? We give our friends, families, bosses, and clients the best of us, but God gets whatever is left in our tank, which is often not much. In Nehemiah, we see that we are expected to give the best of ourselves—the first of everything. That means we tithe before we pay our bills. We pray before we start our day. We remember that God should be the biggest priority in our lives, not the leftovers. What do those leftovers look like in regular life?

"I would read my Bible, but I'm just too busy."

"Did you have time to eat today?" I ask.

"Yes, of course."

"Why do you feel the need to eat?"

"If I don't eat, I would get sick and die."

"Exactly."

The same is true of our spiritual lives. If we do not feed our souls, they will also die. We must make our spiritual body the same priority that we make our physical body. However, keep in mind that quality is better than quantity; it is more beneficial to meditate on a single scripture throughout the day and have that Scripture's meaning soak in, than it is to read a chapter a day and not really take in the information. God wants our hearts and our minds, not just our time. Think of your body. What would be better? Three meals of ice cream or one big meal of chicken and vegetables? If you can read a few chapters a day and really absorb the material, that's ideal, but don't rush it. Don't read X-number of pages just so you can say you read them. Don't read more than you can absorb just because your friend is reading more than you are.

God is royalty. Give Him your sincere best.

Jesus is the King of Kings, and He is coming over. He will be in your home. What are you serving Him?

Thought:

"When we resist God, we draw near Satan" (Beth Moore).

Action Step

Spend time talking to the King of Kings. Give him the best of you.

_____

_____

_____

_____

_____

_____

_____

_____

_____

_____

Passion 2015 – Draw Near
https://www.youtube.com/watch?v=ikWJaSlF6Rw

Video Recommendation:

Memorize:

"Let us draw near with a true heart in full assurance of faith, with our hearts sprinkled clean from an evil conscience and our bodies washed with pure water" (Hebrews 10:22).

Pray

Dear Lord, forgive me for giving You my leftovers. Help me to give You the best of me—the best of my heart, my soul, and my time. Give me more time in my day. Amen.

Write your own prayer:

_____

_____

_____

_____

_____

_____

_____

_____

_____

_____

~ DAY 3 ~

JUST KISSES?

THEME: Surrender
READ: Job 1

Do you love chocolate? I absolutely love chocolate, way more than I should. Imagine your hands are open, and I give you a chocolate Kiss. I give you the option: You can eat that treat, or you can give it to someone else. Over the years, I have done this illustration with many people. Some will give it away with expectation. Others give it away begrudgingly. And then some just simply keep it. Whoever has the empty hands gets a large chocolate bar.

This is the meaning of this illustration. God has amazing things for us. He is looking for empty hands to fill. If we hold onto the small things in life, we may miss out on the larger things He has for us. Often we are asked to give something to someone else, and we do so begrudgingly or maybe not at all. God is not able to bless us as He would like to. Part of faith is trusting God enough to have open hands—to believe that when we surrender to His will, He is ready to bless us.

I have witnessed pastors in ministries that is dying, who are not willing to step down. Two things happen in this scenario: The church is not blessed, and another person who could flourish in the position is not being given opportunity. We need to give away our Kiss so that everyone benefits. Loss is not always bad. Most times, it is about getting something better.

Job has one of the most tragic tales in the Bible. I love Job's attitude at the end of Job 1. He praises the Lord, despite his loss.

When God takes things out of our lives, He always returns it better than before.

In 2010, I surrendered my life to God, and I lost everything—my house, my car, my job, my ministry, my church, all within a few months—but in 2011, I got it all back and it was better than before. The path I was on before was not the right one. This was a redirect that brought me to where I am today. None of that would have happened, if I hadn't surrendered everything. It is a faith thing. We need to surrender what we have so that God can bless us with His ultimate plan. What are you holding onto that you need to surrender?

Thought:

"There are no levels of surrender. Either we surrender or we don't" (Author unknown).

Action Step

Think about what you may need to surrender to God and then symbolically put out your hands and leave it with Him.

_____

_____

_____

_____

_____

_____

_____

_____

_____

_____

Hillsong – Surrender
https://www.youtube.com/watch?v=s7jXASBWwwI

Video Recommendation:

Memorize:

"I appeal to you therefore, brothers, by the mercies of God, to present your bodies as a living sacrifice, holy and acceptable to God, which is your spiritual worship" (Romans 12:1).

Pray

Dear Jesus, please forgive me for anything that I am holding onto that You have specifically encouraged me to get rid of. Give me the strength to surrender this thing to You, and the faith to receive the blessing You have for me in the future. Amen.

Write your own prayer:

_____

_____

_____

_____

_____

_____

_____

_____

_____

~ DAY 4 ~

IT'S A MARRIAGE

THEME: Relationship with God
READ: Revelations 19:1-10

Once upon a time, there was a couple who got together. Everyone was super excited for them. The guy and girl had an amazing relationship, and things appeared to be going great. At first, they were telling everyone about one another. They went everywhere together. If you saw one of them, you almost always saw other one. But as time went on, the woman got a new job and was often "too busy" to hang out. Overtime, she stopped calling or texting him as much. They maybe got together once a week for an hour or two, and when they did have a chance to talk, it was usually in short spurts without any real substance. Eventually, it became too hard, and they broke up.

In contrast, there is an older couple who have been married for more than fifty years. They talk every day and do almost every hobby together. Their mannerisms are similar. They laugh at the same things and seem to share a secret language. Most of the time, they will finish each other's sentences and do not even have to ask the opinion of the other one. Over time, they even seem to look like each other. They spend most of their life together talking about everything, and have truly become *one*.

The Bible equates our relationship with Christ as a marriage. If we are like the first couple where we only spend time with Jesus for an hour or two on Sundays, and we hardly ever talk to Him, we will not have a powerful relationship. We will barely know Him, and over time, the relationship will be die. In contrast, if we spend lots of time with Him, the closer we will become. The more we spend with Him, the more we'll act like Him. We'll pick up His mannerisms; we'll think like Him, and see things the same way He does. If we want to be like Christ, we have to work on our relationship with Him. That means spending time with Him daily, not weekly. As James 4:8 states, "Draw near to God, and He will draw near to you."

Thought:

"If you spend no personal time with God, you cannot say you know Him personally" (Becka Goings, 2013).

Action Step

Make a plan. Schedule a time. Find a place. Make God a priority.

Hillsong UNITED – Whole Heart
https://www.youtube.com/watch?v=eRUM7oCPYls

↑ Video Recommendation: ↑

Memorize:

"Draw near to God, and He will draw near to you."
(James 4:8).

Pray

Dear Lord, help me to find quality time in my day to spend time with You. To work on my relationship and make it a priority. I pray that we will be stronger and more in tune.
Amen.

Write your own prayer:

_____

_____

_____

_____

_____

_____

_____

_____

_____

_____

~ DAY 5 ~

READ THE RECIPE

THEME: Reading the Bible
READ: Psalm 119

I love cake. Especially chocolate cake. So, let's make a cake together. Here is the recipe and everything we need:

Ingredients
2 cups all-purpose flour
2 cups sugar
2 teaspoons baking powder
1 1/2 teaspoons baking soda
1/2 cup vegetable canola oil, or melted coconut oil
2 large eggs
1 teaspoon salt
1 teaspoon espresso powder
3/4 cup unsweetened cocoa powder
1 cup milk buttermilk, almond, or coconut milk
2 teaspoons vanilla extract
1 cup boiling water

But what if I don't want to use all the right ingredients? Instead of flour, I use cream of wheat. After all, it's still wheat right? And I don't have sugar, but I have Pixie Stix. Everyone knows that Pixie Stix are straight sugar, so it could work. And I don't have cocoa powder, but I do have cocoa-flavored cereal, so we'll toss that in there. Hmm, and I don't have baking soda, but I do have soda pop. And oil... there is oil in Italian dressing, right? And instead of eggs, how about chicken bouillon? After all, they are both from chickens.

OK, you get the idea, as silly as it is. If we mixed all of this up, it would taste disgusting. I know, because I have done this illustration many times for youth groups. There is always someone willing to try it and he (it's usually a "he") struggles to keep it down.

The Bible is our recipe book. We are called to follow it as it was written. But often, we like to substitute it with our own ingredients. But it is God breathed, and the infallible Word of God should not be exchanged or rewritten to fit our needs. If we want to start living a powerful life for God, we have to begin with reading our Bible daily and following its words. Not to follow the Word will produce a life that we'll struggle to keep down—a life God did not intend. "Oh, taste and see that the Lord is good!" (Psalm 34:8, ESV). The life God wants for us tastes good. No substitutions required.

Thought:

"Learning is the heart of discipline. You can't just take up your cross daily. You need to take up the Bible every day." (Mark Batterson).

Action Step

Make a plan for reading your Bible. Pick a book to start with or download a Bible list online or go buy a Bible in a Year. There is no right or wrong way to read the Bible, you just need to read it.

_____

_____

_____

_____

_____

_____

_____

_____

_____

_____

Mercy Me – Word of God Speak
https://www.youtube.com/watch?v=4JK6osCH74

Video Recommendation:

Memorize:

"Oh, taste and see that the Lord is good!"
(Psalm 34:8).

Dear Lord, help me to find time to read Your Word and live
according to its standards. Thank You for giving us
direction and I pray that I follow it all the days of my life.
Amen.

Write your own prayer:

_____
_____
_____
_____
_____
_____
_____
_____
_____
_____

~ DAY 6 ~

GOT PRAYER?

THEME: Power of Prayer
READ: Matthew 26:31-75; Acts 2

It was hard enough that Jesus had to endure the cross, but He had to do so without most of his followers supporting Him. All but one of his twelve apostles deserted Him. Peter, who had arrogantly said he would never leave Jesus, denied Him three times.

Earlier in the night, before the crucifixion, Jesus had tried to get Peter, along with James and John, to pray. But all three of them chose to sleep instead. "Then he returned to his disciples and found them sleeping. 'Couldn't you men keep watch with me for one hour?' he asked Peter. "Watch and pray so that you will not fall into temptation. The spirit is willing, but the flesh is weak'" (Matthew 26:40-41, ESV). Jesus knew they needed to be spiritually ready for what was coming. He encouraged them to pray, not once, but three times. Peter was not "prayed up" and ready for what was about to happen. Have you ever wondered what would have happened if Peter had prayed as the Lord asked him to? Maybe Peter would have had the courage not to deny Christ.

We know from scripture that later in the story, prayer does make a huge difference. The disciples, who had locked the doors in fear of the Jewish leaders (John 20:19), were about to stand in front of thousands and proclaim Truth. After the disciples spent time in prayer on the Day of Pentecost and received the Holy Spirit (Acts 1), they were finally able to exhibit boldness in their faith. Peter got up in front of three thousand people and shared the Good News. People were saved and baptized. This was the same man who was afraid to say that he knew Jesus a short time before. Now, he would die for his faith. In fact, all but the one disciple who did not abandon Jesus would be executed for their faith.

Why did these men go from being cowering rabbits to fierce lions? It all comes back to prayer. Jesus prayed for them. "I will remain in the world no longer, but they are still in the world, and I am coming to you. Holy Father, protect them by the power of your name, the name you gave me, so that they may be one as we are one." (John 17:11 NIV). And then, at Pentecost, when the Holy Spirit was invited to move into their hearts, these men were no longer fearful and were able to speak out in boldness.

You know what else Jesus prayed for? You and me. "'My prayer is not for them alone. I pray also for those who will believe in me through their message…'," (John 17:20 NIV). Prayer is so important that Jesus made sure to do it.

As we face the giants in our life, we have to be praying. Faith always starts with prayer. We live in a dark world with a lot of agendas that go against our beliefs. We need to be praying to find the boldness to make a difference.

Thought:
"If you only pray when you're in trouble, you're in trouble." (Author unknown).

Action Step

Stop reading this and just pray. I dare you to set a timer and pray for more than 30-minutes.

Sanctus Real – Pray
https://www.youtube.com/watch?v=aJ4l4gsvYA

Video Recommendation:

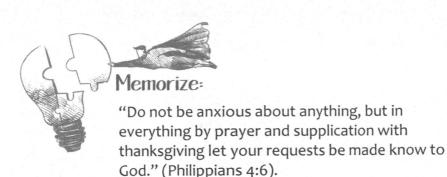

Memorize:

"Do not be anxious about anything, but in everything by prayer and supplication with thanksgiving let your requests be made know to God." (Philippians 4:6).

 Pray

Dear Lord, give me the desire to pray daily. Speak to my heart and give me passion and boldness in my faith. Help me to get to the point where it will become easier to just spend time with You. I pray You are able to do great and mighty things in and through me. Amen.

Write your own prayer:

_____

_____

_____

_____

_____

_____

_____

_____

~ DAY 7 ~

THE LIZARD RACE

THEME: Listening to God Only
READ: John 10:1-21

Once upon a time, there were a bunch of lizards that wanted to have a race up the side of a water tower. All of the animal kingdom came out to witness this bizarre event. This tower was gigantic and would grow pretty hot in the summer sun, but the lizards were not worried. They liked heat. Stubborn, they were determined to make it happen.

As the race started, the animals started jeering.

"You can't do it," one shouted.

"You're going to bake in this hot sun," another said.

"This is so silly. You're going to fall," said a third.

As the animals yelled, one by one, the lizards started dropping off the tower. The more that fell, the more the crowd heckled them. Finally, all but one little lizard had fallen off. For some reason, this lizard didn't seem to mind the taunting and kept going, no matter what anyone said. Eventually, to the astonishment of the crowd, he made it to the top and won the race.

A fellow lizard asked him, "Dude, how did you make it?"

The little lizard pulled out his ear buds and said, "I'm sorry what did you say? I was listening to my music."

In life, there will be tasks that God will want us to do that no one will think we can do or should do. The naysayers will test our faith. When people come against faith, some people fall off and go another way. But we need to stay strong and tune out the world. We should listen to one voice only—God's. Though it can be difficult, we should not have faith in men above God. Men will fail us. If we are doing anything in life to please a man, chances are we are not pleasing the only One we need to please. Jesus talks about the voice of the master. He compares His people to sheep and to Himself as our shepherd. He reminds us that His voice is the one that we should trust. His is the only voice that will lead us in a straight path. Learn to listen to Him alone.

Thought:

"God speaks in the silence of the heart. Listening is the beginning of prayer." (Mother Teresa).

Action Step

Write down what God is telling you to do. Ask yourself whom do you need to ignore.

_____

_____

_____

_____

_____

_____

_____

_____

_____

_____

_____

Marvin Sapp – Listen
https://www.youtube.com/watch?v=Pl742pn7bnw

 Video Recommendation:

Memorize:

"For the Lord gives wisdom; from his mouth come knowledge and understanding." (Proverbs 2:6).

Pray

Lord, help me to listen to Your voice alone. Do not allow me to get distracted by the world and its strong voice. Give me the ability to discern Your heart amongst the noise.
Amen.

Write your own prayer:

_____

_____

_____

_____

_____

_____

_____

_____

~ DAY 8 ~

RECOGNIZING THE VOICE

THEME: Knowing God's Voice
READ: I Samuel 3

Yesterday, we discussed listening to God's voice above all else, but sometimes we don't know how. One thing people often ask is, "How will I know it is from God? How will I know what He wants me to do?" God speaks to everyone differently, but the Holy Spirit can be quite persistent. Samuel could not sleep because God was trying to speak to him. How often I wish God would tap me on the shoulder in the middle of the night and say, "Do this." But that is not usually the case.

More often than not, God speaks loudly in our hearts and minds, where the Voice is there waiting for us to listen. We may perceive actual words from God, as we read in Samuel or He may speak to us through an intuition that we develop through prayer and a deep relationship with Him.

This type of intuition can be called discernment. We can find ourselves without peace when we're on the wrong path. When I made the decision to go into the Army, I had originally signed up to go in the Army Reserves (it was safer and closer to home). I remember sitting in English Lit Class, when I broke down crying. I had this overwhelming feeling that I was supposed to go in the regular service. I called my recruiter that afternoon and told her. Instantly, I had peace. From my experience, even scary things will be accompanied by peace if God is directing you in that direction.

Another way God speaks to us is through the use of scripture. As we read, we are drawn to different passages. Bible verses we have read a million times before all of a sudden have new meaning that is directed at our future.

God can also use dreams and ideas in our mind. We see in the Bible that God often used dreams to direct His people. Even Jesus' earthly father, Joseph, was given a dream with instructions about his coming Son. Do not discount what happens while we are sleeping. God said in the last days that men would dream dreams (Acts 2:17).

God also can use people, but know that, typically, if a person comes to you, it should be confirmation of something you already were thinking, not a new revelation, and not something the person already knew you were thinking. God will usually put the situation in your heart first, maybe as a question, but it will be inside. Unfortunately, there are people who love to say "I have a word from God for you," when in reality they don't. When people approach us with a "word," we need to test their revelations with our own hearts and with scripture. The Lord will never ask us to do anything contrary to his Word.

I had a young person ask me about a job offering that would take them out of church both on Wednesdays and Sundays. They wondered if it was God's will to take this job. It went against scripture of keeping the Sabbath day holy. (I know some situations force people to work on weekends, but I challenged this.) I asked the young man, if you are asking God for His will, would He keep you from going to church? So, the young man waited, and found a much better job with better pay. I believe that God will always direct us in a way that lines up with His Word and who He is.

Though there are many ways God can talk to us, the most important thing to remember is to be open and listen. The more time we spend with God, the more we will recognize His voice.

Thought:

"We often miss hearing God's voice simply because we aren't paying attention." (Rick Warren).

Action Step

Think about what God might be trying to tell you today. Ask yourself, "Does it line up with scripture?" Do you have peace about it?

_____

_____

_____

_____

_____

_____

_____

_____

_____

Hillsong - Be Still and Know
https://www.youtube.com/watch?v=WHATCAvlqQA

 Video Recommendation:

Memorize:

"Your kingdom come, your will be done, on earth as it is in heaven" (Matthew 6:10).

Pray

Lord, help me to know Your voice. Help me to be able to discern when it is the path You would have me travel, and when it is me or someone else's will. Amen.

Write your own prayer:

_____

_____

_____

_____

_____

_____

_____

_____

_____

_____

~ DAY 9 ~

FIND A NEW LABEL

THEME: Freedom in Christ
READ: I Peter 2:9-12; John 8:3-11

One night, God woke me up with this poem. I didn't know what to do with it, so I just wrote it down. In a sense, it is my testimony. It is my journey to a better place. My own spiritual journey has taught me that our past should never define us. That is my hope for all Christians. Here is my testimony:

I am nobody special. Some would like to call me "victim." I would say dreamer, survivor, but never victim. A great life doesn't come from what-if's or what happened...A great life is always moving forward to what will be, not what was. That is how I have lived my life. I was considered "dumb" in grade school, thought to be an "airhead" in high school, and I am now called "Doctor." I was told I would never publish, but I proved them wrong thirty-six times. I have experienced horrific things, but I do not name them, for they do not have power over me. Some would label me a victim for events in my life. I am a pastor, a playwright, a cover designer, a novelist, a veteran, a student, a director, an actor, a wife, a professor, a mother—but never a victim. I am more because I have Jesus. I have become more because I do not answer to defeat. No past will ever define me—I am labeled only by God and my dreams. If you call yourself victim, then that is all you'll ever be. Don't you know that you are so much more than that? Find a new label.

What label are you holding onto? We are defined by our pasts, only if we allow that. People may call you things, but their voices do not matter. What does God call you? His child (John 1:12), His friend

(John 15:15), Redeemed (Romans 3:24), Free (Romans 8:2), Accepted (Romans 8:17), Saint (I Corinthians 1:2), Triumphant (II Corinthians 2:14), New (II Corinthians 5:17), One with Christ (Galatians 3:28), an Heir (Galatians 4:7), Unblemished (Ephesians 1:4), Forgiven (Ephesian 1:7), Workmanship (Ephesians 2:10), Member of the Body (Ephesians 3:6), Bold (Ephesians 3:12), Citizen of Heaven (Philippians 3:2), Chosen (Colossians 3:12) and Loved (I Thessalonians 1:4).

We may call ourselves many things, but that is not how God sees us. God loves to use the broken. He chose a murderer with a stuttering problem to free his people from Egypt (Moses). He chose an adulterer and murderer to rule his people (King David). He chose a prostitute to protect his people (Rahab). He chose a woman who had to be healed of evil spirits and infirmities to be the first New Testament missionary (Mary of Magdalene).

The Pharisees brought a woman caught in adultery to Jesus. We may call her the "Woman Caught in Adultery" but Jesus never referred to her as that. He would call her forgiven and free. It is time that you let God choose you and not the enemy of this world. Begin to embrace how God sees you, so that you may move beyond your past to the amazing things in your future. What is your new label?

Thought:

"God sees us with the eyes of a Father. He sees our defects, errors, and blemishes. But He also see ours our value." (Max Lucado).

Action Step

Write down a label or situation you are holding onto. Then write down the opposite of that label. Give yourself a new label.

_____

_____

_____

_____

_____

_____

_____

_____

_____

_____

_____

Judah Smith – Spoken Word Jesus Loves Barabbas
https://www.youtube.com/watch?v=bU-Rfk24Q

 Video Recommendation:

Memorize:

"… The LORD does not look at the things people look at. People look at the outward appearance, but the LORD looks at the heart." (I Samuel 16:7).

 Pray

Dear Lord, help me to see myself as You see me. Free me of my past and anything that has held me back from Your true forgiveness. Amen.

Write your own prayer:

_____

_____

_____

_____

_____

_____

_____

_____

_____

~ DAY 10 ~

ENOUGH OIL

THEME: God Provides
READ: I Kings 17

One day, during large number of layoffs that happened between 2007 and 2012, I came home without a job. A few years later, my husband came home without a job. During both times, our family never had a day without food on the table or money to pay the bills. All that we lost was all returned back in some mysterious way. Checks began coming in the mail; random checks from obscure places. I had been ministering to one organization for more than two decades and the only time they paid me was during this period. I didn't ask for it, they just gave it to me.

In the story about the widow, we see that the oil did not run dry, and the flour was not used up. God provided. He provides our needs; the oil will flow when necessary. We see earlier in the story that God used the ravens to provide food. The Lord has amazing resources.

One thing to note though: the widow was helping a man of God. Throughout scripture, we see that we are called to give the first fruits of our resources to God. When we do, God blesses us. One action of faith is learning to give to God faithfully and trusting He will return it to us. Malachi 3:10 says it best, "Bring the full tithe into the storehouse, that there may be food in my house. And thereby put me to the test, says the Lord of hosts, if I will not open the windows of heaven for you and pour down for you a blessing until there is no more need." (ESV) This Scripture is one reason we know that our "first fruit" should be ten percent (Tithe means ten percent). So, give your tithe, and God will take care of you and your family.

My husband and I are getting ready to start a ministry. We had applied to a business competition at the local college. The winner would receive $5,000. We really needed that $5,000. But we didn't win. Those around us were quick to remind us that God is still with us and He will provide. So, I went to prayer, believing God would somehow give us the money to finish our project. A few weeks later, we got our income taxes back. Can you guess how much they were? Yep, $5,000. That $5,000 was like oil in a jar. There is no earthly reason why that money should have helped us as much as it did, but God stretched it like He often does. He provided for the 5,000 people on the hillside when they were hungry (Matthew 14), He provided manna (bread) and quail to the Israelites in the desert (Exodus 16), and He will provide for you too. What do you need? Start praising God for that provision now.

Thought:

"Where God guides, God provides." (Author Unknown).

Action Step

Have you given God what is His? If you haven't, write that check today. Have faith that He will take care of you.

_____
_____
_____
_____
_____
_____
_____
_____
_____
_____
_____

Matt Redman – You Never Let Go
https://www.youtube.com/watch?v=NM14VZVuoog

Video Recommendation:

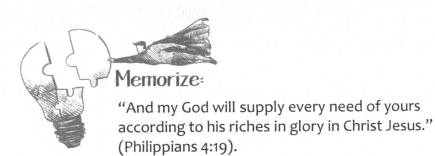

Memorize:

"And my God will supply every need of yours according to his riches in glory in Christ Jesus." (Philippians 4:19).

Pray

Dear Lord, give me the faith to trust You with my finances. Bless the money that I give to You and bless my family. Amen.

Write your own prayer:

_____

_____

_____

_____

_____

_____

_____

_____

_____

~ DAY II ~

BUSTED WINDOWS

THEME: Attitude
READ: II Corinthians 4

Years ago, I drove into the church parking lot with my teen son. I needed to run into my office real quick. I would only be a second. It was a hot day, so I left the car running with the air conditioner on. As promised, I was maybe two minutes, but when I came back, my son was standing in the middle of the parking lot and my car was gone.

Super confused, I quickly tried to assess what had happened. I thought, maybe some of the teens in the youth group moved it as a joke. I said as nicely as I could muster, "Honey, where's my car?"

He turned around and pointed down the parking lot. There it was against a tree. Apparently, the van had rolled down the slight hill, hopped a curb, and hit the tree. The entire back window was busted out. Normally, I probably would have been angry, but I had just come back from a women's retreat and my head was on right. I instantly saw the blessings. First, my son had jumped out and was not in the car when it rolled back and collided with the tree. So, he wasn't hurt. Second, there was tree. Behind that tree was a canyon full of houses. Houses that may have had people in them. Had that tree not stopped the car, the accident could have been a lot worse. And lastly, I had just received an unexpected check in the mail that paid the cost for the window replacement.

When trials happen, we need to focus on the blessings, not the trial itself. Focusing on the trial lets the devil win, focusing on the blessing gives God glory. I love verse 8 and 9 this week, "We are hard pressed on every side, but not crushed; perplexed, but not in despair; persecuted, but not abandoned; struck down, but not destroyed." It is about our perspective. It is about our focus. It is about our attitude. We need to remember that God has us even when things go poorly.

Thought:

"Trials in life are not meant to make us fail, but to see how far we can fly." (Author unknown).

Action Step

Think of a trial you've had to endure; now write down all the blessings around that trial. Then thank God for those blessings.

Israel & New Breed – Trading My Sorrows
https://www.youtube.com/watch?v=-xXiSvddlfA

Video Recommendation:

Memorize:

"We are hard pressed on every side, but not crushed; perplexed, but not in despair; persecuted, but not abandoned; struck down, but not destroyed." (II Corinthians 4:8-9).

Pray

Lord, help me to focus on the blessings rather than the trial. Thank You for those times when things looked bleak but You protected me. Amen.

Write your own prayer:

_____

_____

_____

_____

_____

_____

_____

_____

_____

~ DAY 12 ~

THE ARTIST'S INTENT

THEME: Perspective
READ: Jeremiah 18:2-6; Job 10:8-12

Before the Industrial Revolution, most artists had a limited point of view. When transportation opened up, so did the world of creative subjects, which eventually turned into modern art. One of the rising artists in that time was Kazimir Malevich. In 1915, he painted a red square on a white canvas. At first glance, one might say it's a silly painting. A red square? Come on, my five-year-old could paint that. But if you begin to study it, you will notice it is not a perfect square. One side is slightly crooked. The more you study it, you begin to discover that the square represents communism and the meaning behind this painting is that communism is flawed.

Art is about perspective. It is about knowing the whole picture, the intent of the artist. "Then the Lord God formed the man of dust from the ground and breathed into his nostrils the breath of life, and the man became a living creature" (Genesis 2:7, ESV). We are walking-and-breathing art, and our creator (God) is the ultimate artist. We were made from clay, and we are His masterpiece.

I know there are times we look at our lives, and we just see a blob of paint on a canvas. We wonder why we might have been created and why things are happening as they are. If we want to know the artist's intention, we have to talk to Him. We have to trust Him. He has the answers; after all He created us with purpose and design. People may look at us and just see a flawed square, but when God looks at us, He sees treasures in jars of clay (2 Corinthians 4:7). To understand God, we are often told to approach

Him like a small child. Think of a small child approaching his or her parent with his or her freshly colored picture. The child does so with excitement, and the parent receives the child with the same level of excitement. That is how God sees us. He is proud and excited about His artwork and there are no mistakes.

Thought:

"... hold your head up high, knowing that God is in control and he has a great plan and purpose for your life." (Joel Osteen).

Action Step

Draw or paint your life in an abstract form. What does it look like? How would you explain it? What do you think God intends for that form? If you haven't asked Him yet, ask Him.

_____

_____

_____

_____

_____

_____

_____

_____

_____

_____

Tauren Wells – Known
https://www.youtube.com/watch?v=xckDgX8xNfg

Video Recommendation:

 Memorize:

"For we are God's handiwork, created in Christ Jesus to do good works, which God prepared in advance for us to do." (Ephesians 2:10).

 Pray

Lord, help me to see myself as You see me. Help me to begin to see and believe in the purpose You have for my life. May I also treat others in the same way, as we are all Your creation, and deserve that respect. Amen.

Write your own prayer:

_____

_____

_____

_____

_____

_____

_____

_____

_____

~ DAY 13 ~

WHEN EVERYTHING STOPS

THEME: Complacency
READ: Numbers 13-14

Mr. Barnes got up every morning and went to his job at the factory. Not exciting, but it paid the bills. To add to the dreary job, everyone often complained about the work. Their backs ached, their fingers hurt, the management didn't understand, the conditions were hot, on and on went the complaints. One day, people were complaining so much, that no one was working. The machines were empty, the production halted. What they didn't know was that the management had met only a few days before and decided, if production was "up this month," everyone would get a bonus. But now, production was definitely going down, and instead, there could be layoffs. Mr. Barnes was caught in the situation, and he too would miss out on his bonus.

Complaining and complacency are counter-productive to anything we are trying to accomplish, and especially to what God is trying to accomplish. They halt us, mainly because complaints keep our focus on the wrong thing and not on God. Many blessings and prayers are not answered because people are complaining rather than praying. Think about it, complaining is not against the people you are complaining about, but is actually against the Lord (Exodus 16:8). The Lord directs our paths and brings certain circumstances and people into our lives. If we are always complaining, are we thankful? Think of it this way: If you gave multiple gifts to people, and they complained every time you did so, how would it make you feel? Would you continue to give gifts to those people, or would you eventually stop gift-giving and leave them to endure the consequences of their ungrateful attitude? Everything we have, every time we wake up and breathe, is a gift from God. While God will never abandon us, and will always love us, sometimes, He has to allow us to bear the consequence of our own freewill choice. To use our factory illustration, if we are complaining more than being thankful for His gifts, we may find ourselves facing lay-offs rather than receiving bonuses. God created even our enemies. Rather than focus on what we don't like, we should focus on what God can do. Even the worst circumstances can be for our good, so we really shouldn't complain about any situation.

We see throughout the Old Testament that God was angered by complacency. Just like the employees in our factory illustration, the Israelites did not get the big bonus. Because of their complaining and lack of faith, the Israelites were stuck in the desert and did not get to see the Promised Land. Philippians 4 encourages us to be content in all circumstances. To trust God with other people and situations, and not let our hearts divert to evil. As Jesus instructed, "But I say to you, love your enemies, bless those who curse you, do good to those who hate you, and pray for those who spitefully use you and persecute you, that you may be sons of your Father in heaven; for He makes His sun rise on the evil and on the good, and sends rain on the just and on the unjust." (Matthew 5:44-45, NKJV).

Thought:

"I hate to see complacency prevail in our lives when it's so directly contrary to the teaching of Christ." (Former President Jimmy Carter).

Action Step

Write down different things that you complain about. Then reflect on ways you can turn those things over to God. Pray for the leadership, the people, and the situation.

_____
_____
_____
_____
_____
_____
_____
_____
_____
_____

Matt Redman – Unbroken Praise
https://www.youtube.com/watch?v=hpvJDyLI07M

Video Recommendation:

Memorize:

"Do all things without grumbling or questioning." (Philippians 2:14).

Pray

Lord, help me to have a good attitude with the circumstances around me. Please protect me from those who may harm me and help me to pray for those who persecute me. Amen.

Write your own prayer:

_____

_____

_____

_____

_____

_____

_____

_____

_____

_____

~ DAY 14 ~

CROSSING THE BRIDGE

THEME: Trusting God with our Life
READ: Hebrews 12:1-2; Psalm 16

You know the moment in a movie where one of the characters has to cross a rickety bridge in the middle of a jungle? There is always a missing slat, and the waters are far down—with rocks jutting out—rushing in torrential waves, making it even scarier. Almost always, someone yells out, "Whatever you do, don't look down." And like clockwork, the person looks down, and is instantly terrified. But they still have to cross the bridge. There is something on the other side they need to get to or maybe they are fleeing what is on their side. Whatever the reason, they need to take this brave step.

Imagine for a moment that Jesus is on the other side of the bridge, and He is beckoning you to cross the bridge to join Him. He tells you there is something on His side that will be life-changing, but in order to get there, you have to trust Him and go across this terrifying bridge. He promises you'll be OK. In true form, He says, "Don't look down, just keep your eyes on Me, and I will direct your path." But instead of obeying, you look down, and now you're afraid to cross. Your focus drops to the rocks (i.e. the trials of life). In truth, if you would just keep your eyes on Jesus, He would tell you where to step to keep from falling. But a lack of faith and the distractions of your circumstances prohibit you from experiencing all that God has for you on the other side.

Does any of this sound familiar? How often do we shift our focus from God to our problems? God has amazing things in store for us, but our focus is drawn to our bills, our health, our bad relationships, etc. and we find ourselves waning in our faith. We focus on what *is*, rather than what *could be*. That distraction affects our movement toward something better. If we could just stop looking at the problem and focus on Jesus, He will direct us through the pitfalls and to the other side.

Thought:

"Focus on giants, you stumble. Focus on God, your giants tumble." (Author unknown).

Action Step

Ask yourself, what is under my bridge that distracts me from Jesus? What can you do to get your eyes back on Jesus?

_____

_____

_____

_____

_____

_____

_____

_____

_____

_____

Lincoln Brewster – While I Wait
https://www.youtube.com/watch?v=NswPPVgMaPE

 Video Recommendation:

Memorize:

"For those who live according to the flesh set their minds on the things of the flesh, but those who live according to the Spirit set their minds on the things of the Spirit." (Romans 8:5).

Pray

Lord, help me learn to trust You more. To not be so focused on the problems that I forget to turn to You to help me with them. Amen.

Write your own prayer:

_____
_____
_____
_____
_____
_____
_____
_____
_____
_____

~ DAY 15 ~

NEW THOUGHT ON PRAYER

THEME: True Faith
READ: Mark 4:35-41; Matthew 14:15-21

Jesus and the disciples had a long day of ministry. They climbed into a boat to sail to the other side, away from the crowds. On their way, a huge storm with enormous waves began to break. And where was Jesus? He was asleep in the boat. The disciples instantly started freaking out.

They wake Jesus and accuse, "Don't you care that we are going to drown?"

Another story I've read hundreds of times is the story about the feeding of the five thousand. The disciples came to Jesus and said, "It is already past time for supper, and there is nothing to eat here in the desert; send the crowds away so they can go to the villages and buy some food." Jesus tells the disciples to feed the people, and the disciples respond that they merely have only five loaves and two fishes. What I am about to reveal has completely changed my prayer life.

The reason Jesus was frustrated is that in both stories, the disciples approached Jesus with complaints and worry, not with faith. Think for a moment, what would have happened if the disciples had instead tapped Jesus on the shoulder said, "Hey Jesus, the storm is getting pretty bad, would you be willing to stop it or slow it down some?" Or if they brought the five loaves and two fish to Him and said, "Here is what we have, would you please feed the masses?"

Instead, they were looking at the problem, not at the Person who held the solution. True faith sees that Jesus has the solution. We just need to ask instead of whine. If your boss is giving you a hard time, instead of saying, "God why do you have me here? I can't stand it." Why not pray, "God please, either change his attitude or mine, or move me?" Instead of saying, "I don't like the way our church is going," why not pray, "God help the pastor to listen to your heart and if my heart is in the wrong place, change it." We need to be more proactive in our prayers. We need to stop focusing on what is happening, and start focusing on what God can do about it.

This problem has been going on a long time. In the Old Testament, we see the Israelites complaining about the Egyptian forces hot on their tail. This response from Exodus 14:11-12 is classic:

> They said to Moses, "Was it because there were no graves in Egypt that you brought us to the desert to die? What have you done to us by bringing us out of Egypt? Didn't we say to you in Egypt, 'Leave us alone; let us serve the Egyptians'? It would have been better for us to serve the Egyptians than to die in the desert!

The people are saying that they would rather be in slavery, than to trust and see what God would do. What if they had said, "God, please protect us from the Egyptians"? What a difference faith makes. True faith believes that God will take care of it, which means worry cannot be a part of that scenario.

Thought:

"Worrying doesn't change anything, but trusting God changes everything." (Author unknown).

Action Step

Take a moment to ask yourself, what are you complaining about? Have you truly trusted God with the outcome? How could you pray differently?

_____

_____

_____

_____

_____

_____

_____

_____

_____

_____

Jeremy Camp – Walk by Faith
https://www.youtube.com/watch?v=fQMUa96ZTHA

 Video Recommendation:

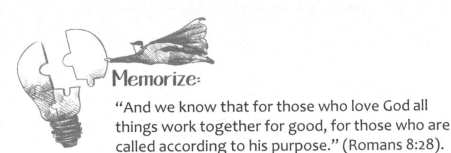

Memorize:

"And we know that for those who love God all things work together for good, for those who are called according to his purpose." (Romans 8:28).

Pray

Lord, help me to trust You when life is scary or chaotic. Let me come to You with the problem, rather than complain about what is happening, and trust You with the solution. Amen.

Write your own prayer:

_____

_____

_____

_____

_____

_____

_____

_____

_____

~ DAY 16 ~

MISSED RESCUE

THEME: *Trust*
READ: Deuteronomy 1

A man named Simon who was out to sea. He got caught in a horrible storm, but he didn't fear it, because he trusted God. The ship was wrecked, but he swam to the shore of a small island. As always, he praised God for taking care of him. Almost immediately, he began to pray for rescue. Days went by, but the man's faith was strong. He prayed harder and longer. One morning, he saw small fishing vessel on the horizon. The owners of the boat rowed ashore. They were rough looking, and Simon was scared. One of them said, "Hey, are you OK? Do you need help?"

Afraid of what these two might want, Simon said, "No, I'm good. God will rescue me."

The two shrugged, returned to their boat, and sailed away.

Simon continued to pray for rescue. Weeks went by. Eventually a helicopter hovered over the island. One of the officers yelled down, "Hey man, do you need a lift?"

Simon had never been in a helicopter. He was too frightened. What if it crashed, after all, he was still traumatized by the shipwreck. He yelled back, "No, thank you. I'm waiting for God to save me."

The helicopter flew away.

A few days later, a small child from a nearby fishing village motioned for Simon to come with him.

Simon had heard many stories about native cannibals. He imagined his head on some stick. Simon shook his head and pointed skyward. "My God will rescue me."

The boy shrugged and left him to his prayers.

Time went on, and Simon eventually died of starvation. When Jesus met him at the gate, Simon was quick to ask, "Why didn't you ever rescue me?"

Jesus replied, "I sent you a boat, a helicopter, and even a local child—I can only help those who help themselves."

"But I was afraid."

"Then you did not trust Me."

You may have heard other renditions of this story. The outcome is always the same. The person does not reap the benefits of God's providence. The principle of in this story happens all the time. We ask for something in faith, but then when it looks different than we thought, or we are afraid of what could happen, we reject it. As we pray, we need to realize that God hears us, but the way in which He answers may come in unexpected shapes and sizes.

I have prayed for new jobs but turned them down due to fear. I've had opportunities to speak or write, but have missed a deadline because I was scared. I even sat on this book for a decade because I was too nervous to finish it. But I am not alone. I have met many men who were called to be ministers but never finished their studies. My mother was one of the most talented people; she could create professional cakes, flowers, dresses, candles—you name it, if it was arts-and-crafty, she knew how to do it, and do it well. When I asked her why she didn't start a wedding planning business, she said, "Oh, I don't think I would ever make it."

It has always made me sad. See, anything God sets up will always come with His provision. We need to be a tuned into what God is trying to tell us or show us.

In Deuteronomy, the Israelites refuse to go into the promised land. This is what they had hoped and prayed for, but their fear kept them from enjoying the blessing. If we are so distracted by what we want, or we are too fearful to grab hold of the opportunities that God places in front of us, we may miss the miracle all together.

Thought:

The only difference between a dream and a reality, success and failure, is that someone stopped trying. (Kimberlee Mendoza).

Action Step

Reflect on anything in your life that you are praying for that God may have answered, but you have rejected the miracle. Is there a faith action that you yourself need to do?

_____

_____

_____

_____

_____

_____

_____

_____

_____

Hillsong Young & Free – *Trust*
https://www.youtube.com/watch?v=En4LGz5N8T8

Video Recommendation:

Memorize:

"And those who know your name put their trust in you, for you, O Lord, have not forsaken those who seek you." (Psalm 9:10).

Pray

Lord, please take away any fear that I have. Help me to follow Your will with boldness. Give me the strength, wisdom, and power to do what You have called me to do. Amen.

Write your own prayer:

_____
_____
_____
_____
_____
_____
_____
_____
_____
_____

~ DAY 17 ~

TRUST THE DETOUR

THEME: God is at Work
READ: Proverbs 3

I was only seventeen when I decided to go in the Army. In order to get into Basic Training, as a woman, I had to be able to do "one man's push-up." Just one. No problem. Before I enlisted, I had trained with a Marine.

The day of the test, they led us into a room with a table. We stood in line and waited. Finally, it was my turn. I climbed up on the table, ready to do a single push-up.

The sergeant squatted next to me and said, "Go."

I pushed one out.

"Lower," she said.

I did another one.

Once again, "Lower." And again, and again, and again. Pretty soon, my skinny arms had pushed out dozens, and I fell to the table.

"Fit Co!" she said. (*Fit Co.* was short for "Fitness Company" where "would-be-soldiers" do physical training for eight hours a day for two weeks.) Being put into Fit Co. delayed my permanent assignment and didn't allow me to progress with the friends I had met. They would go on without me.

In that moment, I was furious with God. I yelled at Him, "How could you bring me all the way out here, just to do this to me?"

All the friends I had made in the past week went onto basic training, and I shipped off to *two weeks* of hades on earth. They dropped me to do push-ups for everything. "You looked at me funny. Drop and give me twenty." "You stepped on a crack. Push out fifty." "You were the last one to chow. You owe me thirty." I just didn't understand. But I completed my two weeks. On test day, I miraculously pushed out *fifty* man push-ups, mind you, and eventually graduated from Basic Training.

When I got to my training school for my job (I was to be a Chaplain's Assistant), I was *two* weeks late, so they held me back to go into the next class. At first, I was frustrated. But then the class I missed was shipped off to the 1989 Conflict in Panama.

After I graduated from school, I went on to my permanent station, where I was to live and work. I was once again *two* weeks late. I was supposed to go to what they call "Signal Company," but because I was late, they put a different person in my place. Signal Company was the first unit to ship out to Desert Storm. My company did not go.

Twice God protected me from war due to a single man's push-up. I believe that if God can use a push-up, he can use anything. Sometimes we do not see what God is doing. The detour may feel overwhelming, even frustrating, but remember God is in the helicopter and we are in the car. From His viewpoint, He can see far ahead of what we can see. The detours are meant to protect us; we simply need to trust Him.

Thought:

"The detour is God ordained and well worth the journey." (Julie Giordano).

Action Step

Think of the detours in your life and write down how they have been for your good. Ask yourself what detour you may currently be in and how it might help you.

_____

_____

_____

_____

_____

_____

_____

_____

_____

_____

_____

Elevation Worship – *Give Me Faith*
https://www.youtube.com/watch?v=dNwt7LQiYck

↑ Video Recommendation: ↑

Memorize:

"Trust in the LORD with all our heart, and lean not unto our own understanding." (Proverbs 3:5).

Pray

Lord, help me to trust You even when things do not seem to be going my way. Help me to see that You are in the detours and the waiting. Amen.

Write your own prayer:

_____

_____

_____

_____

_____

_____

_____

_____

~ DAY 18 ~

TIMING IS EVERYTHING

THEME: God's Timing
READ: Habakkuk 2:1-3; Isaiah 40

As any woman who has borne a child will testify, that last trimester of pregnancy is a long and arduous three months. The nursery is ready and the additional twenty pounds of baby weight gets old and uncomfortable. A woman will sit in the nursery and dream about holding her new baby. But no matter how much that woman desires to hold her baby, not once would she wish for that baby to come earlier than he or she is supposed to. Why? Because the mother knows the baby would not be fully developed. If the baby comes too early, the infant could be sick and weak. In the last few months, the baby's lungs are forming and fat is building in the baby's skin to keep him or her warm. Every moment in the mother's womb is a productive one.

God's timing is much like a pregnancy. Each moment waiting for God's plan to be born is an opportunity to develop into the person who can handle the future God has for him or her. If we got what we wanted too early, we would not be ready or the position may not be ready.

My husband and I are nine years apart in age. Exchanging stories, we figured out that we were at the same concert when I was in high school. Had I met him then, I would have thought he was old and would probably never have gotten together with him. Timing is everything.

For a while, I had felt called by the Lord to become a college professor. So, when I finished my Ph.D., I thought God would God would make me a college professor, instantly. But it took several years. It was painful, and I didn't understand at the time why my prayer wasn't being answered. But hindsight truly is 20/20. At the same time I was praying for the miracle that would make me a college professor, another woman, whom I had never met, was also praying for a miracle—to get pregnant. That woman was sitting in the chair I would one day occupy. In order for my prayer to be answered, her prayer had to be answered first. When she became pregnant, she stepped down, and her chair became vacant. My door opened. The point is, only God can see the full picture. Only God knows what puzzle pieces need to be moved for our particular miracle to happen. My prayer wasn't being ignored. It was in the process of being answered. God didn't say, "no." He said, "not yet."

If you are praying for something, understand that everything must be ready, including you. God knows the right time; you just have to trust Him. Instead of saying, "Please God, make it happen right away," pray, "Help me to remain faithful and to grow while I'm waiting."

Thought:
"Sometimes arriving too quickly is detrimental. It is dangerous to arrive without our character mature or intact." (Lisa Bevere).

Action Step

Think of what you are praying for. What are some ways that you might prepare for that thing you desire? What might get in the way? Or how might you need to grow for that to happen? Or if someone else is involved, what might God be trying to do in and through him or her?

_____

_____

_____

_____

_____

_____

_____

_____

_____

_____

Kristene DiMarco - Take Courage - HD
https://www.youtube.com/watch?v=r49V9QcYheQ

Video Recommendation:

Memorize:

"For still the vision awaits its appointed time; it hastens to the end—it will not lie. If it seems slow, wait for it; it will surely come; it will not delay." (Habakkuk 2:3).

Pray

Lord, help me to grow and become the person You have called me to be. Prepare me for the future You have in store. Also, help me to be patient until that day comes.

Amen.

Write your own prayer:

_____

_____

_____

_____

_____

_____

_____

_____

_____

_____

_____

~ DAY 19 ~

CLOSED DOORS

THEME: God's Direction
READ: Revelations 3:7-8; Isaiah 43

Many times, I have gotten myself psyched up for a food or dessert, only to show up at the restaurant and find that it is closed. Closed doors are never fun. Especially when those closed doors are attached to something we want or our future. A lot of times, we think we are supposed to go a certain way, but then those opportunities close firmly, and we find ourselves confused, questioning God. But we need to trust and not try to force the door open. That entry is not for us. God has a better door for us to find. It is funny, people will say, maybe God will open a window, but normal people do not climb through windows. That is going somewhere you do not belong. Just wait, God will provide your own door.

My church had service in an elementary school for years. The set-up and tear down and the lack of hours the property was available was exhausting. So, they began to pray for a property. My pastor set his mind on this one church in particular. The proximately to his home was walking distance. It was in the right neighborhood. He just knew this was "the one." He prayed and prayed. It seemed like the owner of the church building was just a prayer away from opening that door. Then one night, that pastor told my pastor, "It's never going to happen."

My pastor sat in his driveway confused and wondering why. Asking what we all ask at times: "Now what?" Instead of getting mad, he began to pray. While he sat there, his cell phone rang.

Someone asked him if he was still looking for a property. The caller's property was bigger. It was better located. Had more parking. In all ways, it was a bigger blessing.

Closed doors are not hammers that are meant to keep us from progressing forward, but rather, they are guides. They are God's way of saying, "Just wait, I have something better for you."

Back to my original story, many times when I found the restaurant closed, I ended up trying a new one that was open. Because of that, I've discovered new places I never would have tried before. Embrace the closed doors. They put you on a path that will be better in the end.

Thought:

"Trust God's timing; He makes all things beautiful in His time." (Sarah Wehrli).

Action Step

Write down the word "better." Tell yourself, God has something "better" than anything you might have for yourself.

Hillsong Young & Free – Hindsight
https://www.youtube.com/watch?v=Uy34gCRgUA0

Video Recommendation:

Memorize:

"The steps of a man are established by the Lord, when he delights in his way." (Psalm 37:23).

Pray

Lord, help me to not get discouraged when I encounter closed doors. Help me to keep praying and trust You with the future You have for me. Amen.

Write your own prayer:

_____

_____

_____

_____

_____

_____

_____

_____

_____

_____

~ DAY 20 ~

GOT TICKETS?

THEME: Preparation
READ: James 1; 2:14-26

Think of some place you have always wanted to visit. Now, imagine for a moment that you have been invited to go with a group of friends. . All you have to do is get the tickets. No big deal because you have the money and the time free. You are super excited. You tell all your family and friends. You blow up social media with the possibilities. You even put up a countdown clock to the big day. Simply put, you can't wait. It will be the most awesome experience ever. Then the day arrives. You're all set to go, but you realize you were so busy talking about the event that you never bought your tickets. In your excitement to go, you didn't pack. You are not ready to go at all, and now it's too late. Those who did prepare will leave without you. Seems ridiculous, right?

Except that is how we often live spiritually. We pray and tell everyone about the miracles God will do in our lives. We plan the perfect future for ourselves, but when we get to the gate, we do not have the ticket to get on. The Bible says, "Faith by itself, if it is not accompanied by action, is dead." (James 2:17). We have to prepare with more than words and dreams.

Consider Jesus. We know from scripture that Jesus could have begun His preaching ministry at age twelve. He was found in the synagogue speaking with authority. Even though this was true, He did not officially launch his ministry until He was thirty-years-old. The King of Kings waited eighteen years to fulfill His purpose as the Messiah. During those years, we know from scripture that Jesus grew and learned. He got prepared. Jesus didn't just build with his carpenter father; He also learned scripture. He had a perfect relationship with His Heavenly Father. That was decades of prep. So, while we are waiting for God's will for our lives to come to fruition, what can we do to prepare? Do you need to go to school or get training? Who do you need to meet? What groups do you need to join? I met someone once who said they wanted to be a nurse. I asked her, "Are you in college?" She said, "No." I said, "Then how will you become a nurse?" I know we talked about this in a prior day, but it is worth coming back to. What are you doing to prepare for God's plan and purpose for your life?

A friend of mine once said, "Get the keys, so when you get to the door, you can open it." God has amazing plans for your future, but you have to do your part. I know people who talk and talk about how they want to be in full-time ministry, but they are not willing to go to college or seminary. They state they are too *busy* to go to school. Or, they'll say, "It just isn't the right time." When *is* the right time? You will wake up ten years from now ten years older with or without the degree or certification. Why not just get it and be ready when God calls you? I have worked two full-time jobs, run five ministries, and had two small kids all while going to school. If you truly want to do God's will, then you have to prepare for what He is calling you to do, whatever that is, whatever the challenges to completing that preparation. If you aren't ready when the call comes, then God will ask someone else. No more excuses. Get your ticket.

Thought:
"By failing to prepare, you are preparing to fail." (Benjamin Franklin).

Action Step

What can I do to prepare for His calling, so that when it happens, I am ready? Write down your calling. Now, write down what it would take to get there. Then write down why you haven't started yet. Now, start.

_____

_____

_____

_____

_____

_____

_____

_____

_____

_____

Upper Room – Teach Me to Obey
https://www.youtube.com/watch?v=F2Jt5C1qm-E

 Video Recommendation:

Memorize:

"Equip you with everything good that you may do his will, working in us that which is pleasing in his sight, through Jesus Christ, to whom be glory forever and ever. Amen." (Hebrews 6:10).

Pray

Lord, I pray that I am preparing for Your plan and that I continue to believe in the purpose You have for my life. If I am misdirected, please realign my thinking to Your purpose. Amen.

Write your own prayer:

_____

_____

_____

_____

_____

_____

_____

_____

_____

_____

~ DAY 21 ~

PAIN FOR PURPOSE

THEME: Trials
READ: Luke 22

There is a great line in the movie, *The Neverending Story*, where one of the characters says, "It has to hurt if it's to heal." To some people, that sentiment may seem strange. We often want pain to just stop. We wonder why God would allow us to walk through something that hurts us so much. But pain has purpose.

Consider the Biblical character Job for a moment—one of the most devastating stories in the Bible, when it comes to torment. He suffered greatly, not just physically, but emotionally and spiritually as well. Thousands of years have gone by, but his story *still* inspires people who walk through hard times.

Another story that is even more important is the suffering of Christ. We see Him in the Garden of Gethsemane begging the Father for another way, to spare Him the pain that was sure to come. Jesus knew that dying for our sins would be painful. The Bible says He was so anguished that He sweated drops of blood (Luke 22:44). But His pain had purpose. Without Him enduring that pain, we would not have received the gift of salvation.

I don't know if you are walking through something painful right now, or maybe you know someone who is walking through trying times—but your or their suffering can have purpose. Sometimes that purpose is simply to challenge our faith. Sometimes the purpose is to get us to where God wants us to go. Sometimes, like Jesus' suffering, it is not even about us, but about others. Whatever the reason, remember Jesus' final part of the prayer, "yet not my will, but yours be done." (Luke 22:42, NIV).

For many things there will be no answer until we get to Heaven. We will probably never understand why children die or bad things happen to good people, but remember that God is always in control and has a plan, even for our suffering. My biological dad was a drug addict and alcoholic who put me in danger many times. I could look on all I suffered during my youth with bitterness, anger, resentment, and self-pity. Instead, I see that through my painful childhood, God gave me a heart to minister to the men of Teen Challenge for over twenty-two years. Even in the darkness, let God have the glory. Seek the purpose behind His allowance for the trials and tribulations.

Thought:

"When you come out of the storm, you won't be the same person who walked in. That's what this storm's all about." (Haruki Murakami).

Action Step

Write down a time when you were in pain, then reflect on what might have been God's purpose for allowing you to go through that pain.

_____

_____

_____

_____

_____

_____

_____

_____

_____

_____

Hillsong United – As You Find Me
https://www.youtube.com/watch?v=RUZ1hAldvkY

Video Recommendation:

Memorize:

"Blessed is the man who remains steadfast under trial, for when he has stood the test he will receive the crown of life, which God has promised to those who love him." (James 1:12).

Pray

Lord, I pray You help me walk through the trials of life with a joyful heart. Please show me Your purpose in the struggle and give me the strength to endure it, and allow me to use the experience for Your glory. Amen.

Write your own prayer:

_____
_____
_____
_____
_____
_____
_____
_____
_____

~ DAY 22 ~

BLIND FAITH

THEME: *Trust*
READ: Mark 8:22-26; John 9:1-7

My son was born blind in one eye. It isn't that his eye doesn't work, but his brain decided not to turn on that part of his body. We have been praying for healing for as long as I can remember. My fear was always that he would not be able to drive. One day, I came across a website, where a person plugs in his or her birthday and it gives one a life verse. When I plugged in my son's birthday, it was the story of Jesus healing the blind man. (But not the instant one, the one where things are blurry at first.) I have thought for sure that meant God would heal my son before he had to take his driver's test.

The day finally came. My son passed the written part of the driving test with flying colors and now it was time for the illustrious eye exam. I shamefully told my 16-year-old son, "If you keep your other eye open behind your hand, you'll be able to see."

My son responded, "Where is the faith in that?"

So, I released him to take the test. I started praying, "Lord, if you plan to heal him, now would be a good time."

My son took the eye test—and failed. I don't have to tell you how I felt in that moment. Frustrated. Let down. Worried.

The DMV has a second test that people take if they fail. He could only miss three on this test. Anything more than that and he would be labeled "visually impaired" and would not be allowed to drive.

He went to the second test. Once again, I began to pray. They tallied his score—he missed exactly three. Enough to pass. My young son turned to me and said, "See Mom, you just have to have faith."

Miracles—we like to define them. To say how they should happen. Many people have been baffled by the Mark 8 account of the blind man. In this story, the man is not instantly healed. After Jesus spits, the man sees blurry people the first time around. The second time, he is fully healed. We know that Jesus could do it outright. In John 9, he put some mud on a man's eyes, and after washing off the mud, the man could see clearly. Why are these accounts so different? Because every miracle is like a fingerprint. It is not "one fits all." I believe that the Mark 8 blind man healing is a reminder that sometimes it takes time.

I also must consider that my son may never be healed. His disability has morphed him into the man he is. We observe this many times in scripture. Moses had a stuttering problem (Exodus 4:10-14), and Paul had a "thorn" (II Cor. 12:6-7). God could have healed both, but rather, He used those weaknesses for His glory, as those men had to rely more on God, which kept His servants humble. The bottom line is that we can't second-guess God or what He will do. In the end, we trust Him. He has a plan, and it will work out.

Thought:
"Never be afraid to trust an unknown future to a known God." (Corrie ten Boom).

Action Step

Think of a time when God worked a different miracle than one you were expecting. Why do you think He chose that path? Do you ever have to ask yourself, "Where's the faith in that?"

_____

_____

_____

_____

_____

_____

_____

_____

_____

_____

Martina McBride – God's Will
https://www.youtube.com/watch?v=YCRrrPoEhPc

Video Recommendation:

Memorize:

"You keep him in perfect peace whose mind is stayed on you, because he trusts in you." (Isaiah 26:3).

Pray

Lord, help me to trust Your plan, even when things do not make sense. Help me to use those things that seem like flaws to others, but will make me stronger in my faith. Amen.

Write your own prayer:

_____

_____

_____

_____

_____

_____

_____

_____

_____

~ DAY 23 ~

WHO IS DOING IT?

THEME: Waiting on the Lord
READ: Psalm 91

For a long time I was trying to get a certain job. I sent out one resume once a day for almost two years (if you do the math, that is more than 600 applications). I was discouraged that I had little to no bites. I shared my discouragement with my family.

My dad said, "God always just gives me a job. I never have to apply for them."

Then my step-mom said, "Yeah, me too. God always just gave me a job."

My sons both pipe in, "Yeah, us too."

My husband nods and adds, "Yeah, the same has always happened for me."

Immediately, I began to cry and admit, "That has never happened for me."

For a second it was quiet, and then my dad looked right at me and said, "That is because you are always trying to do it yourself."

That hit hard. It was true. I had never just waited on God in prayer. I had always been trying to do it. My husband and sons applied to one place after someone had told them about the job. When I had pushed them about applying more, they all had the faith to wait. Faith is an interesting thing. It is about trusting God with our paths. Though we need to do our part, we also need to rest and trust God. It is a fine line. There are people who expect God to do it, and then there are others who try to do everything themselves. Neither is good.

My family still had to apply. They weren't going to get the job simply because they knew about it or were recommended for it. They had to write, call, or go in. Faith without works is dead.

But, then there are people like me who want to make it happen with my own strength. Sometimes, I need to stop, trust God, and *not* try to make it happen. I don't know which one you are, but when you pray, wait for God to tell you what to do.

Thought:
"Sometimes you have to just let go and see what happens." (Author Unknown).

Action Step

Write down what you need to release. Write down a prayer for someone that you have wanted to help and ask God if that is His will.

Michael W. Smith – Lord, I Give You My Heart
https://www.youtube.com/watch?v=JsAKeRyK-xw

 Video Recommendation:

Memorize:

"Humble yourselves, therefore, under the mighty hand of God so that at the proper time he may exalt you, casting all your anxieties on him, because he cares for you." (I Peter 5:6-7).

Pray

Lord, help me to know when to act and when to rest in You. Give me the wisdom and strength to release my life and abilities into Your hands. Amen.

Write your own prayer:

_____

_____

_____

_____

_____

_____

_____

_____

_____

~ DAY 24 ~

THE GREAT BABYSITTER

THEME: God's Timing
READ: Jeremiah 29

Sometimes I will hear preachers say, "I know it is hard when God isn't answering your prayer." This drives me crazy, because God ALWAYS answers our prayers. He just doesn't always say, "Yes." Sometimes He says, "No." And sometimes, He says, "Wait." Maybe we aren't ready or the situation isn't ready. Yesterday, I told you about the 600+ applications that were out in the ether. It was a frustrating time and even after my dad spoke to me, it didn't get easier overnight. Then one day, God gave me this vision of my future as if it were a baby. My "baby" was playing with the Father outside my home. Jesus and I were inside. Jesus was sitting in a chair trying to talk to me, but I was at the window, looking out, worrying about my baby. I was so focused on my future that I wasn't spending time with Jesus.

Finally, Jesus said, "Don't worry about your baby. Father has Him. They'll come in when it is time."

First and foremost, I realized God is probably a pretty good babysitter. He's got it. I know that we often get so focused on the answer to our prayer that we lose the faith to allow God to make it happen. We forget that God holds the universe in His hands, surely He can watch over [insert here what you are worried about]. Our timing is not His timing. True faith believes that God will do the right thing in the right time, always.

People often quote Jeremiah 19:11, but don't always read the rest of the story. When we get into verse 12, we see that it is about us "calling on Him and praying." Verse 13 says to "seek Him with all our heart." The promise is there, but we must do our part and pray. We must trust God with our "baby." He will bring it to pass when *it* is ready; when *you* are ready, and most importantly, when *He* is ready.

Thought:

"It's not can you trust God; it's whether you can trust Him in His timing." (Liz Curtis Higgs).

Action Step

Define your "baby." What are you worried about? Then write down what it will take to surrender that "baby" to God.

_____

_____

_____

_____

_____

_____

_____

_____

_____

John Waller – While I'm Waiting
https://www.youtube.com/watch?v=Bb7TSGptd3Y

↑ Video Recommendation: ↑

Memorize:

"For I know the plans I have for you, declares the Lord, plans for welfare and not for evil, to give you a future and a hope." (Jeremiah 29:11).

Pray

Lord, help me release [insert baby] to You. Help me to trust You and wait on You while You oversee the future.

Amen.

Write your own prayer:

_____

_____

_____

_____

_____

_____

_____

_____

_____

_____

~ DAY 25 ~

SILVER AND GOLD

THEME: Asking God
READ: *Acts 3*

"Silver and gold I do not have, but what I do have I give you: In the name of Jesus Christ of Nazareth, rise up and walk" (Acts 3:6, NKJV). You've probably read this story many times before and maybe even sang the song in Sunday school as a child. It is a great testimony of God's healing through his people. But have you ever considered what would have happened if Peter had had silver or gold in his satchel? What if he had had a great day of fishing and was actually loaded with drachma (coins in Christ's time)? The man would have asked, and Peter would have given the man what he wanted. Likely, the man would have been happy and blessed—for a short time. But his problem would not have been solved. It would have been a temporary fix to a permanent problem.

Often, we ask God for something that is only fleeting. He doesn't give it to us because He knows it won't help us, but we might feel frustrated and ignored. But the reality is, if we had it, it would only satisfy us temporarily. God has amazing things in store for us. That is why rather than ask for all the good things in life, we simply need to pray, "Lord, fill my hands with what You deem best for me. Perform the miracle that fits my situation."

I heard the comedian Michael Jr. once say that he doesn't necessarily give something to a homeless person just because he has something to give. He waits to see if God tells him to, because what if there is a man behind him who is stingy and God is working on that man and wants *him* instead of Michael Jr. to help. I think that is profound. We need to trust God to guide us and not just do actions without direction. We do not know the mind of God. Like most of this devotional book will say, it is about trust. It is about surrender followed by faith.

We need to be in prayer always. Author Jerry Jenkins once asked Billy Graham how he was so successful, and Graham replied, "Because I pray without ceasing." If we are always praying, then we will know what to do and when to do it. We won't have to pray for God's will, because we will already be walking in it.

Thought:

"We are closer to God when we are asking questions, than when we think we have all the answers." (Abraham Joshua Heschel).

Action Step

Think about what you praying for. Ask yourself, would you be OK if the answer was less than what you prayed for?

_____

_____

_____

_____

_____

_____

_____

_____

_____

_____

Lauren Daigle – *Trust in You*
https://www.youtube.com/watch?v=naVFVveJNs

Video Recommendation:

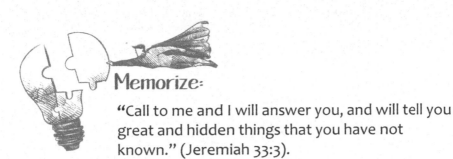

Memorize:

"Call to me and I will answer you, and will tell you great and hidden things that you have not known." (Jeremiah 33:3).

Pray

Lord, help me to know when to act and when to stop. Let me be open to Your perfect will and not to impose my will on the various situations. Amen.

Write your own prayer:

_____

_____

_____

_____

_____

_____

_____

_____

_____

_____

~ DAY 26 ~

EVEN PANTS

THEME: God Cares
READ: Luke 12:22-34

Not so long ago, I really needed to trust God for something, and my faith was slightly lacking. It was my birthday, and my son decided to take me camping for the weekend. We got a late start and arrived at the campground after dark. This particular campground did not have a ranger station or any signage. My son and I didn't know where to go. We were about to climb back into our car, when out of nowhere, this young guy came out of the darkness and told us where to go (up a tall hill in the dark). I honestly do not know if we ever would have found the campground without his help. Interestingly enough, we never saw him again the rest of the weekend, but we were extremely grateful.

The next night, we realized we did not bring enough firewood. Moments after we talked about it, a big log fell out of the tree next to our camp. We were once again grateful. The log meant that we wouldn't have to go to bed at 5:00 PM. In the meantime, we wanted to go on a hike, but my pants kept falling down. I said, "Man, if only we had brought a bungee cord or something, then I could use that as a belt." Moments later, I looked up in the tree, and there was a bungee cord someone had left behind. In that moment, the reality of God being with us that entire weekend became extremely clear. He was there to tell us where to go, he was there to supply our needs, and he even cared about something silly like my pants. He did all this to show me that if He will show up for the minor things, surely He will be there for the big things.

I have heard people say that God does not care about the little things. What we have to understand is that *we* are not "little things." He cares about you and me so much that He suffered and died to redeem us. Because He cares about us that much, He does care about whatever concerns us, whether that thing is little or big. He cared about my direction, and the firewood, and my pants! He also cares about my faith, and finding ways to encourage that is important to Him.

Thought:

"How many of us still live by the phrase, 'if only,' when God has said, 'I already...'" (Author unknown).

Action Step

Write down different times when God has taken care of the little things in your life?

_____

_____

_____

_____

_____

_____

_____

_____

_____

_____

Chris Tomlin – Jesus Loves Me
https://www.youtube.com/watch?v=c8gKXu6J2wE

↑ Video Recommendation: ↑

Memorize:

"Indeed, the very hairs of your head are all numbered. Don't be afraid; you are worth more than many sparrows." (Luke 12:7).

Pray

Lord, please reveal Yourself to me and help me to trust You in all areas of my life. Amen.

Write your own prayer:

_____

_____

_____

_____

_____

_____

_____

_____

_____

_____

~ DAY 27 ~

PARTING WATERS

THEME: Miracles
READ: Exodus 14; II Kings 2:7-8, 13-14

We all have heard the mighty miracle performed by Moses as he raised his arms over the Red Sea. This big miracle saved thousands of lives. Even the secular world is aware of this miracle. But did you know that the prophets Elijah and Elisha performed the same miracle with their coats. Sure it was a tinier body of water and the crowd was a tad smaller, but the exact miracle just the same. Why do you suppose few people talk about it? Both are impressive. Both were done by the power of God.

Often in life, we are so mesmerized by the big and mighty miracles in other people's lives that we neglect to see what God is doing in our own lives. I had been waiting for a miracle for more than nine years. While reading a devotional, the author told me to write down every miracle I had experienced in my life—all the things God had done from birth to now. So I did. I wrote down every one I could think of: I have been healed, protected in a tragic accident, shielded from stupid decisions... The list was long.

When I finished writing them down, I had an urge to read some of my old journals. Sometimes I do that as an encouragement or to remind me of what I've walked through before. I randomly selected a journal from the middle of the pile, which was actually from nine years earlier when I'd first started praying for the miracle. I opened it to the middle page, and there was a list of miracles I had written nine years ago.

Instantly, I understood. The prayer I had started praying nine years earlier was still on God's mind. He brought me to that place for a reason. Someone might try to chalk moments like that up to coincidence, but I think God works in God-instance. I have been keeping journals for more than 20 years. There are thousands of journal entries I could have opened, but God had a specific day for me to see—one that mirrored my then-current day.

Don't focus on other people's miracles, rather, realize the miracles God is doing in your own life.

Thought:

"Some people don't think miracles happen... well, they do." (Forrest Gump).

Action Step

Write down all of the miracles God has ever done in your life.

_____

_____

_____

_____

_____

_____

_____

_____

_____

Jesus Culture – _Miracles_
https://www.youtube.com/watch?v=S-auXYdMSGM

 Video Recommendation:

Memorize:

"For truly, I say to you, if you have faith like a grain of mustard seed, you will say to this mountain, 'Move from here to there,' and it will move, and nothing will be impossible for you." (Matthew 17:20).

Pray

Lord, thank You for all the miracles You have done in my life. Help me to see them as they happen and to be thankful daily. Amen.

Write your own prayer:

_____

_____

_____

_____

_____

_____

_____

_____

~ DAY 28 ~

JUST BELOW THE SURFACE

THEME: God is Working
READ: I Corinthians 2:6-16

When I was a small child, my teacher gave me a paper cup with dirt in it. She said that below the surface was a seed. I needed to water it, and eventually it would grow. I took it home, hopeful for my new plant. I watered it and went to sleep.

I got up in the morning, and it looked exactly the same. Just a cup full of dirt. Had I done something wrong?

I watered it again and watched it. I watched it, and watched it, and yet, nothing happened.

With maturity, we know that plants take time to grow. We also know that just because we can't see it working, does not mean things are not happening beneath the surface. But as a small child, I didn't understand that.

How often do we pray for something and then go to sleep and expect an answer right away?

As a small child, I didn't realize that things were happening under the dirt. I just couldn't see it, and because I couldn't see the progression, I assumed something was wrong.

In the same way, just because we can't see God's hand in a situation does not mean something is not happening. God is lining up the pieces; he is orchestrating change, getting ready to complete his miracle and plan. My son always says, "We are often one prayer away from a miracle."

I've mentioned before that it took several years for my dream job to come true. To make matters harder, things at my then-current job weren't ideal. So, I applied like crazy. I sent out at least one resume a day for two years. You do the math; that is at least 730 applications. I fasted, I prayed, I begged God, and yet, no one answered. All these seeds (applications) felt as if they were just sitting in a pile of dirt with no growth. My youngest son said, "Mom, I think you need to pray more specifically." So, I did. I wrote the following in my journal: *Texas, Christian College, English Professor, and a certain pay.* Within a week of writing that, at least five schools in Texas called me for an interview. One of them was Wayland Baptist University. I have relatives in every part of Texas except the Panhandle (where Wayland is located), so I turned them down and went to the other four interviews. In three of the four, it was just me and another candidate. They all chose someone else.

Discouraged, I said, "I bet I was supposed to go to Wayland." Would you believe that Wayland called me the next day and said, "Are you sure you don't want to come here?"

I did the interview, and I got the job. It was a seed I'd tossed out there. I could not see that it had taken root. It was the one that God watered. I just couldn't see it because I was so focused on what I thought was *supposed* to happen *when* I thought it should. I needed to trust Him and believe that he was at work.

When we pray, we need to wait on God's timing. And a "wait answer," does not mean God is on vacation. God is working on it. We just need to trust Him with the growth. Eventually, His work (aka: His will) springs up and comes to something beautiful. But if we toss out the cup of dirt too soon, we will miss the miracle. God is never late. His timing is perfect.

Thought:

"God changes caterpillars into butterflies...and coal into diamonds by using time and pressure. He is working on you too." (Author Unknown).

Action Step

Write down what seed (the prayer) you have "planted" in God's garden. Consider something things God could possibly be doing right now to prepare you or the answer.

_____
_____
_____
_____
_____
_____
_____
_____
_____
_____
_____

Akesse Brempong – God is Working
https://www.youtube.com/watch?v=OtWh2YYRDSE

Video Recommendation:

Memorize:

"It is God who works in you to will and to act in order to fulfill his good purpose." (Philippians 1:13).

Pray

Lord, thank You for what You are doing in my situation. Help me to have the faith to wait and trust You. Amen.

Write your own prayer:

_____

_____

_____

_____

_____

_____

_____

_____

_____

_____

~ DAY 29 ~

DIDN'T HAPPEN

THEME: Stopped Miracles
READ: Mark 6:1-5; 8:11-13; 15:29-32

When Jesus was on this earth, He performed hundreds of miracles. The Bible says there are so many that the whole world couldn't contain them all. But did you know there are at least three miracles that Jesus didn't do? Here are the reasons why He didn't do them:

LACK OF FAITH:

In Mark 6, we see the town's people in His hometown did not believe and, therefore, they did not get to experience His power.

WRONG MOTIVATION:

In Mark 8, we see people testing Jesus. He had already shown them many miracles, but yet they still were unbelieving and their attitudes were wrong.

GOD'S PLAN:

In Mark 15, the people asked for Him to remove Himself from the cross, but this would have been against God's will.

We know from scripture that Jesus can and will perform miracles in our lives, but we need to have faith, the right motivation, and it has to be according to God's bigger plan. Test your motivation for the miracle you seek. Ask yourself if you truly believe. Lastly, always end your prayers with "if it is according to Your will." Jesus was bold enough to ask in the Garden of Gethsemane if He could forgo "the cup" that would be His suffering and death. He asked for a miracle, but He ended with "but Your will be done." Jesus had to go to the cross. Because God ordained it as the way we could all be saved, there was no other path Jesus could take if He wanted to be in God's will. Sometimes our miracle does not happen, not due to a lack of faith or an impure heart, but simply because it does not fulfill God's plan. We have to trust God who knows the bigger plan. Miracles happen. We just have to wait for the right one.

Thought: "Miracles happen to those who believe." (Author unknown).

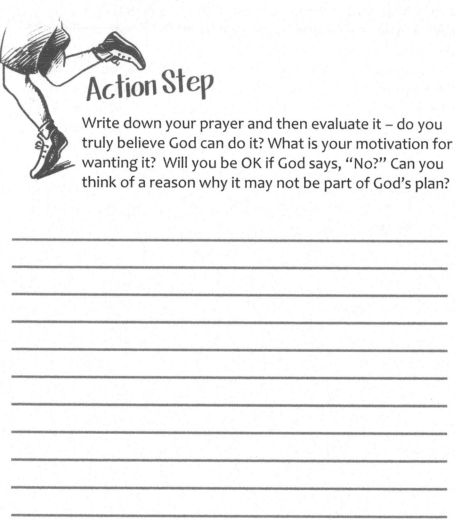

Action Step

Write down your prayer and then evaluate it – do you truly believe God can do it? What is your motivation for wanting it? Will you be OK if God says, "No?" Can you think of a reason why it may not be part of God's plan?

_____

_____

_____

_____

_____

_____

_____

_____

_____

_____

Unspoken – *Miracle*
https://www.youtube.com/watch?v=8yrV9kRr888

Video Recommendation:

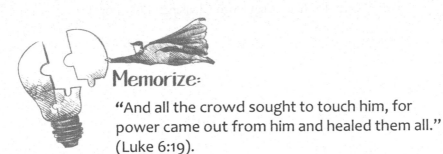

Memorize:

"And all the crowd sought to touch him, for power came out from him and healed them all." (Luke 6:19).

Pray

Lord, I pray that I have the right motivation in my prayers. I pray I have the faith to receive Your miracles. I also pray that I will trust Your final answer, as I seek Your will above all. Amen.

Write your own prayer:

_____

_____

_____

_____

_____

_____

_____

_____

_____

_____

~ DAY 30 ~

UNPLUGGED

THEME: Time with God
READ: Luke 5: 16; Mark 1:35; 6:45-46

When we read these verses this week, we see a trend. Jesus often went off by Himself to pray. He found a secluded place where he could spend time with His Father.

Why do you suppose Jesus did this? Think of your phone. If you used it all day and never plugged it in, what would happen? Eventually, the phone would run out of battery and shut off. Human beings need to do the same. We need to plug into the Source.

Jesus had an active ministry. His physical, mental, and spiritual Self worked hard every day. Sometimes we get caught up in thinking that because Jesus is God, that He was somehow superhuman, but remember that even though He is fully God, the second Person of the Trinity, He is also one-hundred percent human, so He needed to recharge with His Father. Beyond that, He also understood the value of removing Himself from worldly things and having the ability to listen to God. Prayer is a two-way conversation. Without distraction, we can hear the Holy Spirit speak to us. However, with all the distractions, we may not be able to hear His still small voice over the noise.

Not long ago, I was struggling with anxiety. It was bad enough that I was suffering from insomnia, my hands were trembling, and I was getting bad headaches. I went to the doctor, ready for her to tell me I had some horrible disease. Instead, the diagnosis was "stress," and she gave me orders: I was to turn off all technology one hour before bedtime to meditate (pray) and journal.

I needed to be more active in my prayer life, anyway, so now I had the doctor's orders. I followed them, and before long, the insomnia, the trembling, and the headaches started to disappear. But something even more important began to happen. I experienced the peace of Jesus in a powerful way. I started to hear from Him again. It was life altering.

I realized that spiritual and physical things could often be one in the same. There is a reason why God calls us to Sabbath. He knows our bodies need the rest. Like Christ, we need time away from others, time away from the responsibilities of work or school. We need time to talk to our Savior. When we add journaling to our prayer time, it's as if we get a double-dose of grace. Writing our thoughts helps to release all the worries of the day so that our hearts can be emptied of stress; prayer fills in the places where stress was with the Lord's good stuff. I challenge you, even when these forty days are over, to try it. It will be life changing.

Thought:

To pray does not mean to listen to oneself speaking. Prayer involves becoming silent, and being silent, and waiting until God is heard. (Soren Kierkegaard)

Action Step

Find a secluded place (a prayer closet). Turn off your computer, your readers, your cell phone, and your television one hour before bedtime and spend time journaling and praying.

_____

_____

_____

_____

_____

_____

_____

_____

_____

_____

New Life Worship – Here in Your Presence
https://www.youtube.com/watch?v=Aq8P5i9U7-g

Video Recommendation:

Memorize:

"I will meditate on your precepts and fix my eyes on your ways." (Psalm 119:15).

Pray

Lord, let me find time to spend with You. I pray for peace in my life as I give my stress and time to You. Amen.

Write your own prayer:

_____

_____

_____

_____

_____

_____

_____

_____

_____

~ DAY 31 ~

REDIRECT

THEME: Getting Back on Track
READ: Jonah

I am notorious for getting lost. It doesn't matter what trip I go on, I will have to make a U-turn at some point. My family thought getting me a GPS would solve this issue, but it hasn't. On every trip, at some point, I will hear from my Austrian GPS voice, "redirecting," because I missed a turn.

Recently, I was talking with someone about finding God's will. He asked, "What if I make a mistake and don't do what God is calling me to?"

From my experience, God is a bit like a GPS. He has a path for our lives. If we make a wrong turn, He will do everything in His power to get us back on track.

Look at Jonah. He walked away from God's plan, and God found a way to bring him back to his calling by using rough weather, the fear felt by the other men on the boat, and a big fish that swallowed Jonah whole.

I pray none of us ever has to get to the point that God has to take such drastic measures to get us back on track. God wants us to be obedient, but should we ignore or deny His will, He will do everything to bring us back to a place of obedience and the purpose He has chosen for us. God is bigger than our decisions. God is bigger than our mistakes. Just know that the redirect is not always comfortable.

Another way to look at this, is that Jesus is our shepherd. If you have ever read of shepherds, they have a staff with a hook on it. As a sheep is trying to go out of bounds, the shepherd puts out his staff and slowly redirects the sheep to go the right way. God is directing us; we just have to let Him.

Another way to look at this is that God is in the helicopter, and we are in the car. There are detours in our lives that may be frustrating because we cannot see beyond them, but God has a bird's eye view. He sees the pitfalls in our lives and tries to get us to go around them. If we are stubborn and try to plow through the detour, we may find ourselves stuck in a large hole. We need to trust God is guiding us. Like the rest of this book (if you haven't noticed), it is about trusting God.

Thought: "As we keep or break the Sabbath day, we nobly save or meanly lose the last best hope by which man rises." (Abraham Lincoln).

Action Step

Think of a time when God redirected you. What are the ramifications of that redirection? Write down where you think God may want you to go now? Are you on target?

_____

_____

_____

_____

_____

_____

_____

_____

_____

_____

Jonah Movie – God of Second Chances
https://www.youtube.com/watch?v=YeOnADmkD74

 Video Recommendation:

Memorize:

"Commit your work to the Lord, and your plans will be established." (Proverbs 13:24).

Pray

Lord, I pray that I am listening to Your words. Help me to be obedient and trust You. Forgive my sins and help me to move towards the path You have set out for me. Amen

Write your own prayer:

_____

_____

_____

_____

_____

_____

_____

_____

_____

_____

_____

~ DAY 32 ~

SENDING A CLOUD

THEME: Drought
READ: I Kings 18

In the 1930's, America experienced one of the worst droughts in its history. The Dust Bowl, also labeled the "Dirty Thirties," affected more than 50,000,000 acres of land. Due to poor soil management and a lack of rain, enormous dust clouds plagued Oklahoma. You know that these poor families were on their knees praying for rain. A drought is scary and the cure is something that is out of mankind's hands. It must involve a move of God.

In I Kings 18, we see another drought. Elijah was praying for rain. He believed God would answer it. So much so, he kept sending his servant up a mountain looking for this evidence.

Up and down the man went. Again and again, the same answer over and over. Seven times to be exact. I don't know about you, but I think I would have given up on the third jaunt up the mountain. My son used to make me climb this huge hill. Just once up, and my legs were burning and my chest was heaving. One time up, and I was done, let alone seven times. But faith, true faith, will push us out of our comfort zone and propel us to crazy things. The man obeyed and up he went up and down, and finally he saw a cloud the size of a fist. When the man reported this to Elijah, the man of God didn't keep praying; he started running. Why? Because he knew that God was getting ready to pour out his miracle.

You may have experienced a drought in your spiritual life or you are waiting on a miracle that has not come. Notice Elijah didn't wait to see if it would happen, he was active—first, by having faith enough to keep his servant looking for a cloudburst; second, by running as if a major storm had arrived, even when the cloud was just the size of a fist. You have to believe God is getting ready to pour out his rain on your life. It may be as small as a fist at first, but it will come. "Faith is having confidence in what we hope for and assurance about what we do not see." (Hebrews 11:1).

I have a cat that had feline AIDS. It is a non-curable disease that causes fevers and sores on their paws, neck, and ears. My cat was miserable. For over six months, we took her to the vet every three weeks to get a steroid shot just to help her function. One day, my cat jumped onto my lap while she was covered in sores and running a temperature. I put my hand on her and asked that God heal her.

And he did.

She hasn't had sores or fevers for almost a year.

Around the same time, my daughter-in-law found out she was pregnant. The ultrasound showed that my grandson would have water on the brain. When I prayed, God said to me, "Surely if I can heal your cat, I can heal your grandson."

And he did.

My grandson came out healthy and happy.

God used the small miracle of healing my cat to prepare me for the big one of healing my grandson. Remember, even in the small things, God is at work. Sure, it may only be a small cloud, but it is a cloud. Have faith, your cloud is coming. And when it arrives, run towards your miracle praising God for His goodness.

Thought:

"I asked for light, God gave me the sun. I asked God for water, God gave me rain." (Unknown).

Action Step

Spend a half-hour just worshiping God in prayer and song. Not asking for anything, just worshipping Him.

_____
_____
_____
_____
_____
_____
_____
_____
_____
_____

Elevation Worship – There is a Cloud
https://www.youtube.com/watch?v=oZkmDqk2ivs

Video Recommendation:

Memorize:

"Faith is having confidence in what we hope for and assurance about what we do not see" (Hebrews 11:1).

Pray

Lord, I pray that You rain down in my life. I am trusting You for a miracle in circumstance or in my life. Help me to recognize our cloud when it comes. Amen.

Write your own prayer:

_____

_____

_____

_____

_____

_____

_____

_____

_____

_____

~ DAY 33 ~

THREE P'S

THEME: Temptation
READ: Matthew 4:1-11; Matthew 19:16-26

I have heard many people comment, and have thought it myself, that the temptations of Christ didn't seem like real temptations that we face every day. But I studied each one and found that they, in fact, are three temptations that we face on a regular basis. I call them the "three Ps".

The first one was after a forty day fast, and the devil said in verse 3, "If you are the Son of God, tell these stones to become bread."

This is PHYSICAL.

PHYSICAL

A physical temptation can involve food, drink, activity, sex, addictions, anything that would help us feel good, but are only temporary. Jesus answered in verse 4, "It is written: 'Man shall not live on bread alone, but on every word that comes from the mouth of God." He also would say in John 4:13-14, "Everyone who drinks this water will be thirsty again, but whoever drinks the water I give them will never thirst. Indeed, the water I give them will become in them a spring of water welling up to eternal life." Jesus knew the draw of the physical. Too much indulgence to the physical body can cause obesity, depression, addiction, disease, etc. It is why fasting can draw us closer to God. It focuses our attention so we can make

Him the most important thing in our lives. The physical temptation can be one of the harshest to overcome.

The second temptation was in verse 6, "If you are the Son of God," he said, "throw yourself down…"

This one always seemed silly to me until I realized that this temptation is PRIDE.

PRIDE

This is the devil's favorite and biggest issue. It was the very sin that got him kicked out of heaven. His desire for Jesus to exhibit this sin is clear… "you are not better than I am." Pride shows up in our lives in all sorts of ways. Self-centered insecurity, bitterness and unforgiveness, stubbornness are all forms of pride. Like Jesus, we must release our pride and resist the urge to act upon it. That means we must embrace the truth of who we are (our faults and our virtues) and let go of insecurity. We must release bitterness and instead of holding on to mean thoughts and ill wishes about people who have hurt us, we forgive them. We must realize that our way may not always be the only way—or even the *right* way at times— and let go of stubbornness. In other words, we must choose to be humble.

The last temptation was POSSESSIONS.

POSSESSIONS

"All this I will give you," he said, "if you will bow down and worship me" (verse 9). This one seemed truly silly to me, because God owns everything. Even our possessions belong to the Lord. But, then I realized that when God gave Adam dominion (rule) over the earth, God put us in charge of it. And what did Adam do with that responsibility? He gave in to the devil's temptations, and in that way, handed to Satan the ability to rule over the earth. (But only for a little while, Scripture tells us!) But because humanity gave up so much when we sinned originally, we are drawn to want to "own" things, to be powerful and self-reliant. The more money we have, the better cars, the bigger houses, that all seems to equate to more respect and power. So we accumulate possessions, and often we hold them tighter, and are not willing to give them up. We see this in Matthew 19 when the Rich Young Ruler was not willing to give up his riches to follow Jesus. The point of this story was for Jesus to remind us that nothing should be more important than serving God. If they are, they become our idols. God is a very jealous God, and does not want anything to be more important than His love for us… and our love for Him. (Note, jealous in this context is not the same as being envious. One of the dictionaries definitions of jealous is being "protective." We are His children, and He is protective over us. He does not want us distracted by anything other than our relationship with Him. It is that relationship that makes us healthy and joyful. Distractions of the world will only harm us and keep us from being our best selves. And God wants the best for us.)

These temptations are our temptations. We need to combat them the same way Jesus did—in three ways.

Know Scripture

Notice Jesus quoted scripture to combat Satan's taunts. He would not have been able to do that, had He not spent time in the Word of God.

Fast

Jesus spent days without food. Why fast? Fasting is surrender. It shows humility. Fasting places more importance of spiritual things than physical ones. In essence, it prepares us to resist temptation.

Pray

Jesus was "prayed up" when the enemy came to him. We have talked about this already, but it's important enough to repeat. We need to be ready at all times to combat the devil who prowls around like a lion ready to devour us (I Peter 5:8). There are several illustrations in Scripture where prayer made a difference, for example: When the disciples wondered why they couldn't cast out a demon in Mark 9:14-38, Jesus replied that it would take prayer.

So we must hide the Words of God in our hearts (Psalm 119:11), humble ourselves with fasting (Psalm 35:13), and watch and pray so we might not fall into temptation (Matthew 26:41).

Thought:

"A temptation usually comes in through a door that has deliberately been left open." (Author unknown).

Action Step

Write down those things that tempt you. Research some scriptures that might help you overcome those things.

_____

_____

_____

_____

_____

_____

_____

_____

_____

_____

_____

Jeremy Camp – *Overcome*
https://www.youtube.com/watch?v=FqXZDz3eCc

Video Recommendation:

Memorize:

"Submit yourselves, then, to God. Resist the devil, and he will flee from you." (James 4:7).

Pray

Dear Lord, Help me to overcome the temptations in my life and to spend more time with You. Help me to give up those things that have become an idol and allow me to be content in Your presence. Amen.

Write your own prayer:

_____

_____

_____

_____

_____

_____

_____

_____

_____

~ DAY 34 ~

THE SPIRITUAL DIET

THEME: Spiritual Health
READ: Galatians 5

Have you ever watched one of those weight loss shows? They always start with the person eating junk food. Lots of it. Then someone will toss all of it and the person will begin to eat right. They begin to exercise and the weight begins to drop off. The person no longer has to take medication or use a machine while he or she sleeps. Each pound makes it easier to move and do the things he or she wants to do. The change of diet alters his/her life in a positive way.

Our spiritual lives are the same. If we are putting in spiritual junk food (things that do not help our soul like worldly TV, music, movies, etc. that exhibit sinful desires), we will find ourselves struggling spiritually. It will be harder to spend time with God and our attitudes will suffer. But as we begin to toss those things out of our lives, and begin to fill up on spiritual nourishment (worship music, sermons, scripture, etc.), we will begin to feel stronger in our faith.

We think of healthy foods as fruits and vegetables. Jesus often used plants to demonstrate his point, such as parables about wheat and seeds. Also, He cursed the fig tree that was not producing fruit. We are encouraged to have healthy fruits in our lives. "But the fruit of the Spirit is love, joy, peace, forbearance, kindness, goodness, faithfulness, gentleness, and self-control" (Galatians 5:22-23). A truly healthy spiritual body exhibits these in their life.

Fruits of the Sprit

love – There are many definitions and degrees of love, but we are called to love God and others.

joy – Not to be confused with happiness. Happiness is temporary, joy is eternal. Joy comes only from God, and joy is the realization that God is with you, no matter your circumstances.

peace – This comes from the Holy Spirit working in our minds and hearts. We have no fear or worry, but we rest in the knowledge that Jesus Christ is holding us.

forbearance – Other words for this might be perseverance or long-suffering. It is the ability, through the grace of the Holy Spirit, to withstand hard circumstances with endurance.

kindness – Often, compassion stems from this fruit. Moral goodness, integrity and a concern for our fellow man, we act out in a gentle way.

goodness – This is seen in our actions as the Holy Spirit empowers us to work against our sinful natures and seek a righteous life. James 2:26 tells us that faith without works is dead, and the closer we get to the Holy Spirit, the more our outer goodness shows the world the inner goodness we've found.

faithfulness – We work to be true to our commitment to Christ and to others in the Kingdom of God. This is our devotion, our promise, and our pledge.

gentleness – In Greek, this is translated as meekness, not to be confused with weakness. Rather than avowing one's authority or superiority over someone, a gentle person helps, even if the other person doesn't deserve it.

self-control – You probably have worked on this one for the past thirty-four days. This fruit controls one's body and desires through the power of the Holy Spirit.

Thought:
Create a life that looks just as spiritual on the inside as you look on the outside.

Action Step

Looking at the list above, which fruits do you struggle with? Write down ways that you might be able to build them into your life. Also, consider what "junk food" you might be incorporating daily into you spiritual diet and how you might get rid of it.

_____

_____

_____

_____

_____

_____

_____

_____

_____

_____

Donald Lawrence & Co. – *Spiritual*
https://www.youtube.com/watch?v=Ej2yieeD9Qc

Video Recommendation:

Memorize:

"But the fruit of the Spirit is love, joy, peace, forbearance, kindness, goodness, faithfulness, gentleness, and self-control. Against such things there is no law." (Galatians 5:22-23).

Pray

Lord, I pray that I am able to get rid of anything that is not of You. Help me to exhibit the fruits of the spirit in my life.

Amen.

Write your own prayer:

_____

_____

_____

_____

_____

_____

_____

_____

_____

~ DAY 35 ~

POWER IN HIS NAME

THEME: Spiritual Power
READ: Acts 4:1-12

I once heard an incredible story about the power of Jesus' name. In 1432, in Lisbon, Portugal, a terrible plague broke out. It was so contagious, that even touching an item touched by the infected would insure one's death. People were dying everywhere, in homes, streets, and even churches. Monsignor Andre Dias was one of the few priests willing to bravely care for the victims. He began to encourage each of them to write the name of Jesus on cards and keep those with them wherever they went and under their pillows at night. Jesus said to speak His name with their lips and let the name into their hearts.

History shares that God rewarded their faith as they miraculously began to heal. The sick were no longer dying, but were being healed. Within a few days, the city was plague free. It is a testimony of the power behind the name of Jesus. Often we forget and allow the enemy to have a foothold in our lives. Scripture states that demons shudder (James 2:19; Luke 10:17).

Did you know that Jesus is called more than 50 titles in the Bible?

Here are just a few:

Bridegroom (Matthew 9:15)

Cornerstone (Acts 4:11)

Alpha & Omega (Revelation 22:13)

Morning Star (Revelation 22:16)

Author & Perfecter of our faith (Hebrews 12:2)

Bread of Life (John 6:35)
Faithful & True (Revelation 19:11)
Deliverer (Romans 11:26)
Good Shepherd (John 10:11)
High Priest (Hebrews 4:14)
Head of the Church (Ephesians 1:22)
Son of God (I John 5:20)
Lamb (Revelation 17:14)
Servant (Acts 4:30)
King of Kings (Revelation 19:16)
Immanuel (Matthew 1:23)
I am (John 8:58)
The Lamb of God (John 1:29)
Light of this World (John 8:12)
Word (John 1:1)
Truth (John 8:32)
Lion of Judah (Revelation 5:5)
Messiah (John 4:25-26)
Peace (Ephesians 2:14)
Rock (I Corinthians 10:4)
The Way (John 14:6).
Savior (Luke 2:11)
Friend (John 15:15)

Thought:

"Do you realize how much power is in the name of Jesus? When you speak it, demons have to flee! You have that access! Use it." (Isaac Pittman).

Action Step

Consider the list above and write down who He is most to you?

Jesus Culture – Break Every Chain
https://www.youtube.com/watch?v=EtyVdC7E6Wo

Video Recommendation:

Memorize:

"And there is salvation in no one else, for there is no other name under heaven given among men by which we must be saved." (Acts 4:12).

Pray

Lord, thank You for who You are and for the free gift of salvation. I pray I remember to call on You when I am in trouble or discouraged. Amen.

Write your own prayer:

_____
_____
_____
_____
_____
_____
_____
_____
_____
_____

~ DAY 36 ~

UNPACK

THEME: Righteous Living
READ: 1 Timothy 6:11-21

Have you ever had to move? There was nothing like getting to a new place and looking around at the mound of boxes. Sometimes it can be overwhelming. But it can't stay like that, right? Eventually, it has to all be unpacked. As we begin to unpack, it starts to look messy. Sometimes I am tempted to just toss all the stuff back into the boxes and forget about it. But I don't, because I know that if I endure the mess, over time, everything finally gets put in its rightful place. Eventually, the house is tidy and ready for guests.

A lot of times, when we begin a spiritual journey, different realities regarding our attitude start to unpack themselves, revealing things that maybe we would like to keep stored in a dark box. When I went through this myself, God put a huge spotlight on my negative and complacent attitude. I didn't want to face it at first. It was embarrassing and difficult to admit, but eventually, I had to face it if I wanted to go to the next phase. So, whenever I felt complacent, I began to pray for that situation or person that fed my negativity.

Like the moving process, it may feel more comfortable to repack the ugly truth and just forget it, but in order to set up the Lord's house, we need to unpack all the ugliness that keeps us from Him. Unpack things like anger, bitterness, apathy, distrust, depression, complacency, jealousy, or any other attitudes that are less than becoming and do not mix with Christ's "décor". We cannot get to where we want to go, if we aren't willing to be honest, transparent, and real with God. It will be messy—maybe even painful—for a little bit, but eventually we will have everything in our spiritual lives tidily in order, and we'll see an amazing and beautiful dwelling.

God uses the messed up. Remember, it is our flaws that keep us humble. God could have chosen someone without a temper and a loud mouth to build his church, but he chose Peter. Though Peter struggled with his flaws, those were the qualities that God used for enable Peter to witness to thousands of people. Those qualities made Peter most effective. Jesus helped Peter realize and unpack his flaws so that Peter could learn humility and through that humility, realize how much he needed to stay close to Christ. When Peter tried to keep Jesus from His mission, Jesus spotlighted Peter's flaw by saying, "Get behind me Satan" (Matthew 16:22-23). Peter denied Christ three times, but then Jesus spotlights Peter's flaw and his repentance by asking Peter three times, "Do you love me?" (John 21). Both of those instances were humbling to Peter, but look at the first thing that happened after Jesus' crucifixion: The flawed, but humble, Peter helps to save three thousand people (Acts 2:37-41).

Thought:

"Till sin be bitter, Christ will not be sweet." (Thomas Watson).

Action Step

Write down what attitudes may not be Christ-like, then make a list of ways you might overcome those attitudes.

Tamela Mann – *Change Me*
https://www.youtube.com/watch?v=8m8Ivi4Gu-I

Video Recommendation:

Memorize:

"If we confess our sins, he is faithful and just to forgive us our sins and to cleanse us from all unrighteousness." (I John 1:9).

Pray

Lord, I pray that You will reveal those things that I need to unpack and help me to draw closer to You and seek righteousness. Amen.

Write your own prayer:

_____

_____

_____

_____

_____

_____

_____

_____

_____

~ DAY 37 ~

NO CONDEMNATION

THEME: Forgiveness
READ: Romans 8

Faith comes in all forms. We have discussed many elements of faith and how to grow in it. Now we will look at faith in our salvation. When I was a kid, the church hammered the idea of the rapture in our heads. Every sermon reminded us of it. We watched movies like *A Thief in the Night* and *Distant Thunder* that showed people disappearing in the blink of an eye. The church preached condemnation: turn or burn, get saved or get French-fried. We believed that if we did not live every second without sin, we would miss Jesus when He came for his church. So, every time the altars were open, we were all down there confessing our sins—just in case.

One night when I was about twelve or so, I finished up in the shower and went to find out about dinner. As I walked through the living room, the television was on. I walked in the kitchen and there were pots boiling on the stove, but my parents were nowhere around. Instantly, I started sobbing. I just knew I had missed the rapture. When my parents returned from talking to the neighbor they were surprised to find me hysterical, in the fetal position, on the couch. Looking back now, I can laugh about it, but at the time it was devastating.

Growing up with that kind of fear often made me doubt my salvation. I John 1:9 states, "If we confess our sins, he is faithful and just and will forgive us our sins and purify us from all unrighteousness." We need to have faith that this verse is true.

That once we ask Jesus into our lives, if we continue to follow Him, we are His.

A pastor once told me that the only time God remembers our sins is when we remind Him. Isaiah 43:25 states, "I, even I, am he who blots out your transgressions, for my own sake, and remembers your sins no more." Yes, when we do sin, we need to ask for God's forgiveness, but not out of fear, rather out of love for Him and sorrow that we've done something that saddens Him, and out of a sincere desire to do the right thing.

We need to trust in Christ's grace to forgive us of our sins and walk in confidence and freedom. As long as we're breathing, He will *always* forgive us when we're truly sorry. Always. No exceptions! "Therefore, there is now no condemnation for those who are in Christ Jesus." (Romans 8:1). The bottom line is to do your best to live for Jesus. By His grace you are saved. You are flawed (me, too!), you will make mistakes (me, too), but know He is always ready and willing to take you back.

Thought:

"The enemy works overtime to keep us in shame. He knows if he can keep us in shame, he can minimize our intimacy with God." (Mike Bickle).

Action Step

Write out your testimony of how you came to Christ and how you might serve Him more.

Elevation Worship – *Reckless Love*
https://www.youtube.com/watch?v=Sc6SSHuZvQE

Video Recommendation:

Memorize:

"Therefore, there is now no condemnation for those who are in Christ Jesus." (Romans 8:1).

Pray

Lord, forgive anything in me that is not of You, and help me to accept Your grace and believe in Your power to make me whole and new. Amen.

<u>Write your own prayer:</u>

_____

_____

_____

_____

_____

_____

_____

_____

_____

_____

~ DAY 38 ~

SINK OR FLOAT

THEME: Misplaced Faith
READ: Genesis 6:9-7:24

On April 10, 1912, the RMS Titanic started its maiden voyage across the Atlantic Ocean with 2,435 passengers and 900 crewmembers. The Titanic was designed to be the fastest, most luxurious ship of its kind. It spanned 883 feet and was divided into 16 compartments presumed to be watertight. They bragged that she was "unsinkable." That, of course, turned out to be one of the worst assumptions made in history. As you probably know, at 2:20 AM, April 15, 1912, the Titanic sank into the North Atlantic Ocean. They had too few lifeboats, mainly because the designer thought it would look too cluttered for the affluent guests.

Now let's discuss another famous boat—the biblical Ark built by Noah. It was hardly glamorous. It was probably miserable, filled with animals and livestock for forty days and nights, but it served its purpose. The Titanic's purpose was prestige, and people died in the name of comfort. The Ark's sole purpose was to save mankind. It was a testament of God's grace.

Ironically, professional architects and builders designed the Titanic, but an amateur built the Ark. (Of course, the Ark's architect was the God of the Universe.) Often we misplace our faith in people rather than in God. People often say they do not go to church because people are hypocrites. Yes, people are. But that is not why we go to church. We go to church to learn about God and to build a loving community. Noah had people jeering at him while he built his ship. He didn't listen. He kept his ear to what God told him to do, no matter how ridiculous it may have seemed. It took faith to build a boat when there was no water in sight.

When you know you have a mission from God, ignore the naysayers and those who are not in communication with God. Do you have a ministry that is burning in your heart? Have you been hesitant to start it because of what others are telling you? Do you feel called to start a business? Or build a family? When we know the architect of our "boat," and He is directing us on how to build it, we will successfully make it to our destination. Ignore the people on the shore. Remember in the story of Noah, the naysayers were caught out in the storm without protection, but the one faithful to his calling was saved.

Thought:
"Remember when you do your best, God will do the rest." (Author unknown).

Action Step

Consider what God is telling you to build, and ask what it would take for you to build it?

_____

_____

_____

_____

_____

_____

_____

_____

_____

_____

33 Miles - *Calling*
https://www.youtube.com/watch?v=hBuvALWvmtk

 Video Recommendation:

Memorize:

"And whatever you do, in word or deed, do everything in the name of the Lord Jesus, giving thanks to God the Father through him." (Colossians 3:17).

Pray

Lord, I pray that I listen to Your voice alone. Let me be obedient to Your Word, and not get distracted by others that are outside Your will. Amen.

Write your own prayer:

_____
_____
_____
_____
_____
_____
_____
_____
_____

~ DAY 39 ~

BURN AWAY THE DROSS

THEME: Cleaning Up
READ: I John 3:1-10

Over the past thirty-nine days, we have discussed how to draw closer to God, to know God, and to expect great things from God. As we finish this journey tomorrow, it is my hope that you have a renewed fire ignited in you. What is your story? What testimony do you have to share?

Faith without action is dead. If you have a fire burning, it should have purpose. A fire without purpose is usually destructive or it just goes out. Fire fighters will often burn a controlled fire to clear out dead brush. When this is done, the land will eventually become healthy, ready to grow and develop into something beautiful.

The Bible talks about burning away the dross. Dross is defined in the dictionary as "rubbish or anything that is worthless." As we near the end of the journey, what could you burn away in your life? As we begin to step forward in renewed faith, our fire should bring us to a place of passion for the Lord, but if anything is still in the way, it will prevent us from being our best. Be honest with yourself (and with God).

Sometimes it isn't that bad, it just stands in the way. I can remember I used to have a guilty pleasure TV show that I loved to watch. I would leave mid-week service early so that I could get home to watch this show. God really convicted me. I wasn't staying to pray or allow God to move in my life—over a TV show? So I had to give it up. I found that within a few weeks, I didn't care about that TV show any more. We all have things that make us too busy or distort our thought processes. Sometimes they are really difficult to get rid of due to their addictive nature. Sometimes they are just a one-second decision. No matter what, if you know God is calling you to toss it in the fire, you need to be obedient. God is more interested in your soul than your immediate, worldly happiness. Anything more important than Jesus is an idol. Our God is a jealous God and desires that there be nothing more important than His love for us. If it is not drawing you closer to Him, then it is time to release it. If you can't release it, then ask yourself why.

Thought:

"A sum can be put right: but only by going back till you find the error and working it afresh from that point, never by simply going on." (C.S. Lewis).

Action Step

Write down anything that you still need to purge from your life. Then write down what you will do to make that action step.

_____

_____

_____

_____

_____

_____

_____

_____

_____

_____

Hymn: All to Jesus I Surrender
https://www.youtube.com/watch?v=7x2IpLSfqp8

Video Recommendation:

Memorize:

"No one who is born of God will continue to sin, because God's seed remains in them; they cannot go on sinning, because they have been born of God." (I John 3:9).

Pray

Lord, give me the ability to get rid of anything in my life that is not of You. Reveal those things in my life and take away the desire to have them. Amen.

Write your own prayer:

_____

_____

_____

_____

_____

_____

_____

_____

_____

~ DAY 40 ~

CLOSE TO THE ROCK

THEME: Relationship with Jesus
READ: II Samuel 22

Have you ever been rock climbing? I was pretty fearless when I was younger, but I was slightly afraid of heights. That was until the Army made me climb up enormous towers out in the middle of the forest. I soon found a love for it. So much so, that I was willing to do it on my day off. One weekend, I went mountain climbing with my friends. Strange that we did it without ropes and safety equipment. Kind of nuts, but we were young and stupid (I don't recommend you do anything so dangerous). One thing I learned pretty quickly is that I needed to stay close to the rock. If I didn't, I risked falling.

Jesus is the Rock in our life. (I Corinthians 10:4). As we come to the end of this journey, it is important that we set up boundaries for ourselves. A spiritual journey is not successful if it is just a forty-day moment in time that does not change how we spend time with God. The real change comes when the journey is over.

Fire is fierce. It is hot. It is powerful. A faith on fire is powerful. Have you ever been camping and started a fire? In order to keep it burning, you have to do what? Feed it. To the initial spark, you add kindling. Then, as that takes off, you add in more wood, and it starts to grow huge and hot. If you stop feeding it though, what happens? Eventually it burns out. Hopefully, the last forty days have been logs on the fire of your soul. It is my hope that you are now hot and burning and ready to make a difference. This is easy when you are ingrained in a commitment, but what happens now that

that is over? What you've learned needs to become a lifestyle, not just a mountaintop experience. You need to continue to read your Bible, pray, fast, and work to grow your faith.

As kids, we hold up our fingers and sing the song, "This little light of mine, I'm going to let it shine. I won't let Satan blow it out. I'm going to let it shine." The way to assure that your fire will still be burning is to continue to stay close to Him. It is the only way to continue to have a torrid faith. One of the best ways to preserve fire is to light another fire.

So, my last words of advice are: If you aren't involved already, get involved in ministry. Share your faith with others. If you have ever seen a forest fire, they are usually started by one small ember. No matter whether you are a spiritual raging fire or just a slow smolder, you have the ability start something big that will burn through your community. It only takes one to start a revival.

May the Lord bless you and keep you.

Thought:

"May God so fill us today with the heart of Christ that we may glow with divine fire of holy desire." (A. B. Simpson).

Action Step

Figure out what is next: What scripture do you want to tackle? What devotional can you buy? What small group can you join? What changes do you need to implement to stay on fire for Christ?

_____

_____

_____

_____

_____

_____

_____

_____

_____

_____

Hillsong Worship – So Will I
https://youtu.be/yTf9RpzKguU

Video Recommendation:

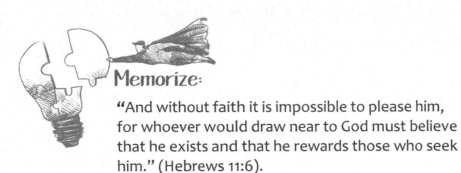

Memorize:

"And without faith it is impossible to please him, for whoever would draw near to God must believe that he exists and that he rewards those who seek him." (Hebrews 11:6).

Pray

Dear Lord, as I end my forty-day journey, I pray that I have the strength to continue to grow and draw closer to You.
Amen.

Write your own prayer:

_____
_____
_____
_____
_____
_____
_____
_____
_____

FINAL TEST

Take a moment to take this test again and see if you see any improvement:

1. I usually...

   a. Read my Bible every day for more than twenty minutes
   b. Quickly read my Bible right before I go to bed
   c. Fit my devotion time in if I have a free moment
   d. Don't ever really read my Bible

2. I find...

   a. I talk to God like He's my best friend for a good amount of time
   b. Sometimes I can only pray for five to ten minutes
   c. It is often difficult to find things to say during prayer time
   d. I never really talk to Him except when I have a problem

3. Which one of these makes your heart flutter more?

   a. Going to a church revival on a week night
   b. Hanging out with friends
   c. Watching sports or TV
   d. Partying

4. Reading a devotional book...

   a. Changes my way of thinking
   b. Isn't something I do often
   c. Puts me to sleep

d. What's a devotional?

5. I have trouble with my mouth (cussing, gossiping, etc.)...

    a. Never
    b. Rarely
    c. Sometimes
    d. Always

6. Giving up the most important thing in my life for God...

    a. Is easier every time, because I know the fruit of what will happen
    b. Stings a bit, but I'm trying
    c. Hurts and I'm not sure if I can do it
    d. Not sure, I've never tried it

7. Prayer to me is...

    a. As essential as eating
    b. Important, but I need to do more
    c. Is something I do when I have problems
    d. Something I don't do

8. If the pastor were to ask me to give up fast food and hobbies for three days, I would say...

    a. Sure, I could use it
    b. I'll pray about it
    c. Sorry, can't right now
    d. Forget it

9. When someone asks me to pray for them, I...

    a. Start right then and there
    b. Usually pray for them once or twice
    c. Say I will, and then never do
    d. People don't ask me to pray for them

10. I am reading this book because...

    a. I'm just so on fire for God; I can't wait to get closer to Him
    b. I know I need to change
    c. Someone told me to or I was curious

d. I feel guilty

TALLY YOUR ANSWERS

Total number of A's: _____
Total number of B's: _____
Total number of C's: _____
Total number of D's: _____

CHECK YOUR FIRE LEVEL

If you had mostly A's, you are burning hot for God, so now go and ignite others.

If you had mostly B's, you're warm, but you have the right heart and with a little stirring of the ashes, you could ignite a blazing fire

If you had mostly C's, you are lukewarm. Look at the questions you marked with C's and D's, and go back through the workbook and see if you can work on those specific things.

If you had mostly D's, you are still cold. I highly recommend talking to a pastor, mentor, or other spiritual leader. Be honest, transparent, and real about where you are at. Sometimes to start a fire when need help.

FINAL REFLECTION

Answer the following questions for yourself:

How have I changed?
What changes do I want to see happen in my spiritual life?
What is my spiritual plan now?

DR. KIMBERLEE R. MENDOZA
Author Bio

Kimberlee R. Mendoza is a wife and a mother of two adult children. She has recently moved from San Diego, CA to Plainview, TX to take on the role of Dean of Language and Literature at Wayland Baptist University. Kimberlee travels throughout the year to various locations to speak. She is a credentialed minister and has been in active ministry for more than 30 years. She is a long-time young adult author and young adult mentor. She also moonlights as a cover artist for The Wild Rose Press. In addition, she won presenter at the CITI Conference in 2016, she is the recipient of the "2006 Sherwood Eliot Wirt Writer of the Year Award," and her poem "Silent Amour" won Creative Arts and Sciences' Editor's Preference Award of Excellence. She has a Ph.D. in Leadership and Higher Education, an MA in Humanities with an emphasis in literature and writing and has just completed her MFA in Writing. She has published various books, plays, and poems over the years, specializing in young adult fiction.

Journal published: Engaging Generation Z: A Case Study on Motivating the Post-Millennial Traditional College Student in the Classroom

US-China Foreign Language and Sino-US English Teaching Journal No. UCFL20190309-1 (2019)

Novels published by The Wild Rose Press: The Hidden Two (2018), The Lost Few (2017), Confessions of a Con Man (2016), The Forgotten Ones (2013), Fried, Scrambled & Unequally Yoked (2009), Wish Upon a Rock Star (2009), Oh Brother, You're Not My Keeper (2008), Seek Ye First My Heart (2008), Love thy Sister; Guard thy Man (2007/2016), Trick to Treat (E-book), The After-School Question (E-book)

Novels by Pelican Book Group: Dark Cognitions (2014), Taps to the Soul (2009), Wanted: Boyfriend for Christmas (2008), A Girl Named Christmas (2007), Reveille of the Heart (2006), Uncharted Waters (E-book), & Lilly's Garden (E-book)

Plays published by Meriwether Publishing: California Bonez and the Stone of Karawan (2017), Who Got the Sherriff? (2014), A Knock Around the Block (2013), Christmas Night Live (2013), The Heart of Christmas (2012), Art to Die For (2012), The Last Pirate of the Caribbean (2010), Mission: Easter (2010), Capisce? (2009), 'Twas the Time Before Easter (2009), Who Dun Stole the Bride? (2008), Shooting Star at Studio 66 (2007), The Case of the Show Stopping Nun Nabber (2005), & The Mystery of Montley's Manor (2003)

Play and Workbook published by Youth With A Mission (YWAM): *The Woman* (2005)

Script published in the *Acorn Review*: *On the Couch* (Sketch, 2002)

Non-fiction book published by Meriwether Publishing: *The Human Video Handbook* (2007)

Poems: "Enjoy Each Day" Motherhood *Memories*. Lotus Books. (2004). Pg. 107.

"Lil' Hands" *Acorn Review Literary Magazine*. Grossmont College. (2000-2001). Pg. 33

"Silent Amour" Creative Arts and Sciences (1993).

"Natural Love Ends" *Language of the Soul Anthology*. Creative Arts & Sciences Enterprises. (1991). Pg. 155

"The Computer Ate My Heart" *Forgotten Moments Anthology*. International Library of Poetry. (1991). P. 171

Flash Fiction: "The Peanut" (2020) Every Day Fiction https://everydayfiction.com/

The Torn Slipper (2022)

Memoir Essay: "November 13, 2009" (2020) The Past Ten https://www.past-ten.com/home/tag/Kimberlee%20Mendoza

Non-Fiction:

Teaching Squirrels: How to Reach Generation Z and Create Lasting Engagement (2021)

Level Up Workbook: Gaining the Skills to Write at the College Level (2022)

Thank you

We appreciate you reading this Crossover Books title. For other titles, please visit our on-line bookstore at www.pelicanbookgroup.com. For questions or more information, contact us at customer@pelicanbookgroup.com.

Crossover Books is
an imprint of Pelican Book Group
www.PelicanBookGroup.com

Connect with Us
www.facebook.com/Pelicanbookgroup
www.twitter.com/pelicanbookgrp

To receive news and specials, subscribe to our bulletin
http://pelink.us/bulletin

May God's glory shine through
this work of fiction.
AMDG